Religion and Life Issues

for WJEC Religious Studies Specification B

Revision Guide

Gavin Craigen
and Joy White

HODDER EDUCATION
AN HACHETTE UK COMPANY

The Publishers would like to thank the following for permission to reproduce copyright material:

Photo credits **pp.3**, **5** True Love Waits (www.truelovewaits.com), **p.29** *Medicine*, *computer* and *house* © Photodisc/Getty Images, *mobile phone* © Milos Luzanin/iStockphoto.com, *food* © Morgan Lane photography/iStockphoto.com, *people watching TV* © 2009 photolibrary.com; **p.33**, **35** *t* Photolibrary Group Ltd/Photodisc, *b* iStockphoto.com/© Lucwa; **pp.51**, **53** NASA.

Although every effort has been made to ensure that website addresses are correct at time of going to press, Hodder Education cannot be held responsible for the content of any website mentioned in this book. It is sometimes possible to find a relocated web page by typing in the address of the home page for a website in the URL window of your browser.

Hachette UK's policy is to use papers that are natural, renewable and recyclable products and made from wood grown in sustainable forests. The logging and manufacturing processes are expected to conform to the environmental regulations of the country of origin.

Orders: please contact Bookpoint Ltd, 130 Milton Park, Abingdon, Oxon OX14 4SB. Telephone: (44) 01235 827720. Fax: (44) 01235 400454. Lines are open 9.00–5.00, Monday to Saturday, with a 24-hour message answering service. Visit our website at www.hoddereducation.co.uk

© Gavin Craigen and Joy White 2010
First published in 2010 by
Hodder Education,
An Hachette UK Company
Carmelite House, 50 Victoria Embankment,
London EC4Y 0DZ

Impression number   9
Year   2015

Cover photo: Daly & Newton/The Image Bank/Getty Images
Illustrations by Peter Bull Art Studio, Countryside Illustrations and Gray Publishing
Typeset in 12pt Goudy by Gray Publishing, Tunbridge Wells
Printed in India

A catalogue record for this title is available from the British Library

ISBN: 978 0340 975 633

Contents

Introduction

About the examination

The WJEC Specification B Unit 1 explores the impact of religion on life issues.

There are four main topics you will be examined on:

- Topic 1 Relationships (includes issues of love, marriage and divorce).
- Topic 2 Is it fair? (includes issues of justice and equality).
- Topic 3 Looking for meaning (includes issues about God, life and death).
- Topic 4 Our world (explores creation and our place in the world).

In the examination paper each of the four topics has five questions. The same format is repeated in each topic:

- a) questions ask you to explain what religious believers mean by one of the key concepts. Two marks are given for these questions.

> **Exam tip**
> There are six key concepts in each topic. Make sure you are able to explain what they mean with an example.

- b) questions ask you to explain the impact of a religious teaching or attitude. Four marks are given for these questions.

> **Exam tip**
> Make sure you include religious language and terms in order to gain high marks.

- c) questions are evaluation questions where you need to give two reasons why a religious believer might agree or disagree. Four marks are given for these questions.

> **Exam tip**
> Remember to include references to religious teachings or practices in your answer.

- d) questions ask you to describe or explain the religious attitudes, practices or teachings on an issue such as wealth or marriage. Six marks are given for these questions.

> **Exam tip**
> Make sure that you answer from two different religious traditions.

- e) questions are evaluation questions where you need to give a range of reasons or evidence to justify your view. Eight marks are given for these questions.

> **Exam tip**
> You must include religious and moral reasons using specialist language for the highest marks.

You can see examples of each type of question at the end of each topic of this revision guide.

About this revision guide

This guide is broken down into the same four topics of the examination. Each topic includes:

- The Big Picture – this gives an overall view of all you should know and issues you should be able to evaluate.
- Religious and specialist terms you could use in your answers. Definitions of the terms can be found in the Glossary on pages 69–70.
- Key concept explanations – there are six key concepts in each topic.
- Key information on the religious teachings/ attitudes and practices for all the issues required.
- Practice evaluation questions and examples of different viewpoints that could be made.
- Exam tips.
- Activities to check your understanding.

Each topic ends with practice questions for that section. Specimen answers are given with the level awarded by an examiner. This gives you the opportunity to improve the answer using the levels on pages 67–8 to help you.

Topic 1 Relationships

The Big Picture

Below is a summary of the key concepts, religious teachings and human experiences you need to know for the examination.

You need to know these!
The a) questions in the examination will ask you about these key concepts, *and* you should also use them in other questions as well.

What is love?

What is the role and purpose of sex?

What commitments do we have to others?

Is marriage out of date?

How important is the family?

What responsibilities do we have towards each other?

Is it necessary to marry in a place of worship?

Should people be allowed to remarry?

Should remarriage be in a religious building?

Should same-sex marriages be allowed in a place of worship?

Whose decision is it concerning the use of contraception?

Why do some marriages succeed and others fail?

Human Experience questions

Questions like these will be asked in c) and e) questions in the examination.

The religious teachings here *should* be used in b), c), d), and e) questions. You need to know religious teachings for two traditions.

Key concepts to think about ▼

CHASTITY

COMMITMENT

CONFLICT

LOVE

RECONCILIATION

RESPONSIBILITIES

Religious teachings to explore

- Adultery and extra-marital sex
- Sex before marriage
  - Pre-marital relationships
  - Contraception
  - Celibacy
  - Sexual activity and commitment
  - Sex as a gift from God
- Marriage
  - Courtship
  - Religious marriage ceremonies
  - Marriage vows and the meaning of marriage
- Divorce
  - Separation and divorce
- Remarriage
- Same-sex relationships

Religious and specialist terms

On the screen below are some important words you could use throughout the topic. You should be able to use terms from two different religious traditions or two denominations of Christianity. Definitions can be found in the Glossary on pages 69–70.

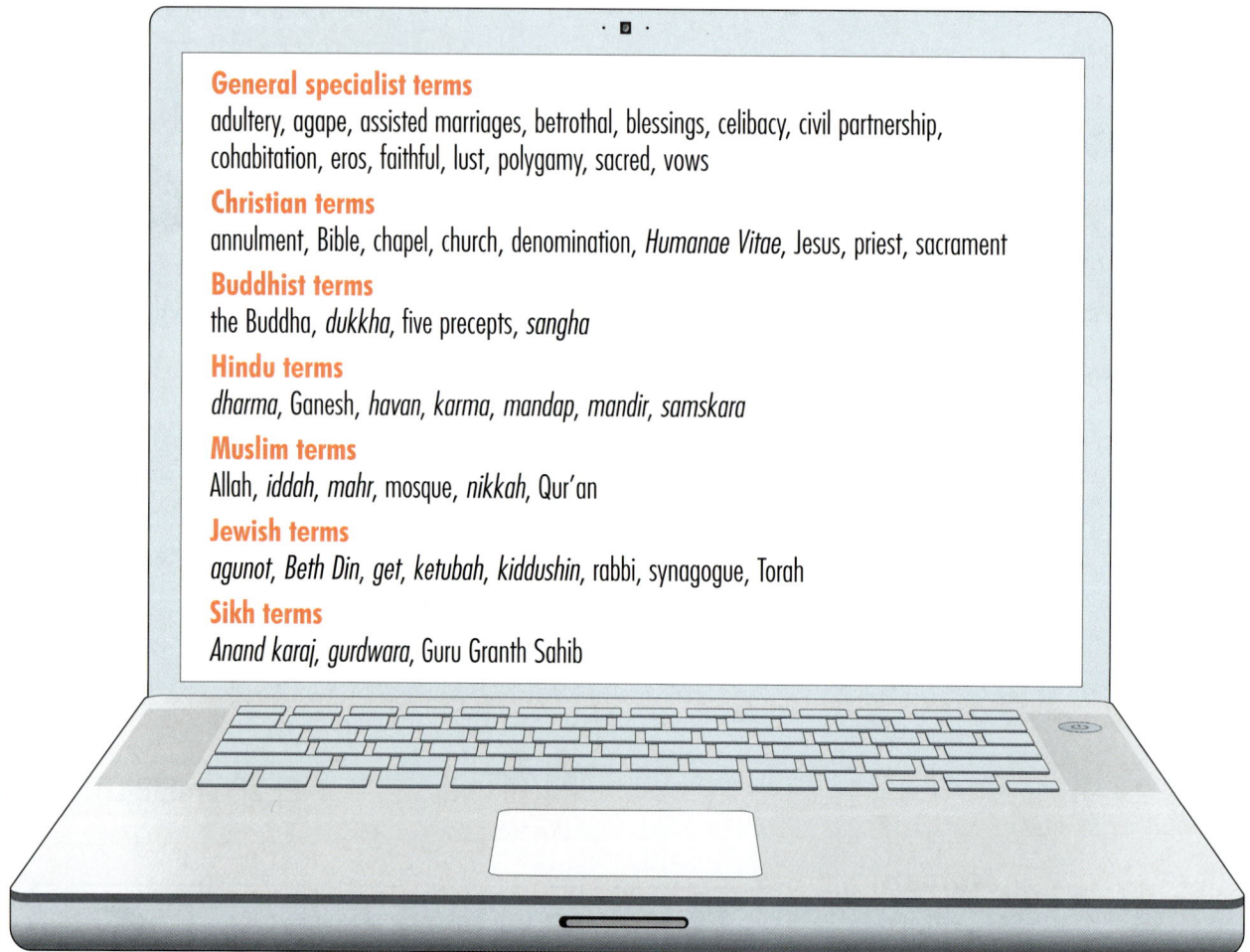

General specialist terms
adultery, agape, assisted marriages, betrothal, blessings, celibacy, civil partnership, cohabitation, eros, faithful, lust, polygamy, sacred, vows

Christian terms
annulment, Bible, chapel, church, denomination, *Humanae Vitae*, Jesus, priest, sacrament

Buddhist terms
the Buddha, *dukkha*, five precepts, *sangha*

Hindu terms
dharma, Ganesh, *havan*, *karma*, *mandap*, *mandir*, *samskara*

Muslim terms
Allah, *iddah*, *mahr*, mosque, *nikkah*, Qur'an

Jewish terms
agunot, Beth Din, *get*, *ketubah*, *kiddushin*, rabbi, synagogue, Torah

Sikh terms
Anand karaj, *gurdwara*, Guru Granth Sahib

Exam Tip

It is important to use general specialist terms and terms from the religions you have studied in your answers to examination questions.

Exam Tip

If you can use stories or teachings from sacred texts to support your answer it will help you get high marks. You don't need to remember the exact words. You can make general references or put them in your own words.

Key concepts

There are six key concepts in this topic. The definition of each is shown in the keys below. The first examination question for each topic (question a)) will ask you to explain one of the key concepts for two marks. You should also refer to the key concepts in answers to other examination questions on the topic.

Commitment — Making and keeping a promise, such as wedding vows.

Chastity — Decision not to have sex before marriage, for example, because it's believed that sex is sacred.

Conflict — Working against each other rather than in unity. Conflict in marriages can lead to divorce.

Love — To have a deep affection and express it through words and actions.

Reconciliation — Apologise or say sorry, and become friends again. Many faith communities have reconciliation services.

Responsibilities — Duties you should carry out, such as looking after family members.

Issues to consider

There are four main areas you will need to know about for this topic:
- issues of love
- issues of sex
- issues of marriage, cohabitation and same-sex relationships
- issues of divorce and remarriage.

Issues of love

There are four issues you should be able to evaluate. These are shown in the diagrams below and on page 7 and are often asked in c) and e) types of questions. Around the four issues in the diagrams are some views (both religious and non-religious) you could include in your answers.

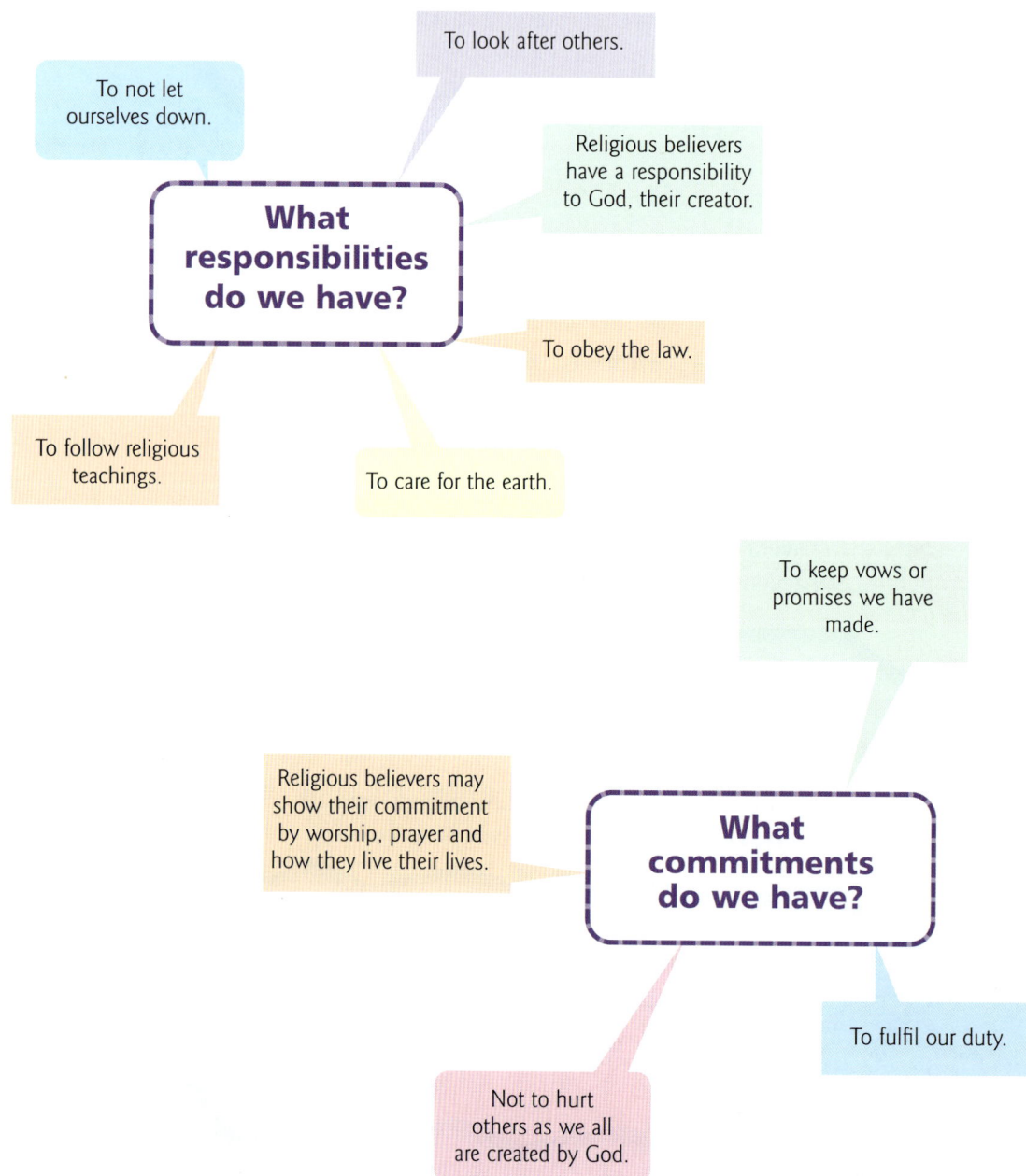

To look after others.

To not let ourselves down.

Religious believers have a responsibility to God, their creator.

What responsibilities do we have?

To obey the law.

To follow religious teachings.

To care for the earth.

To keep vows or promises we have made.

Religious believers may show their commitment by worship, prayer and how they live their lives.

What commitments do we have?

To fulfil our duty.

Not to hurt others as we all are created by God.

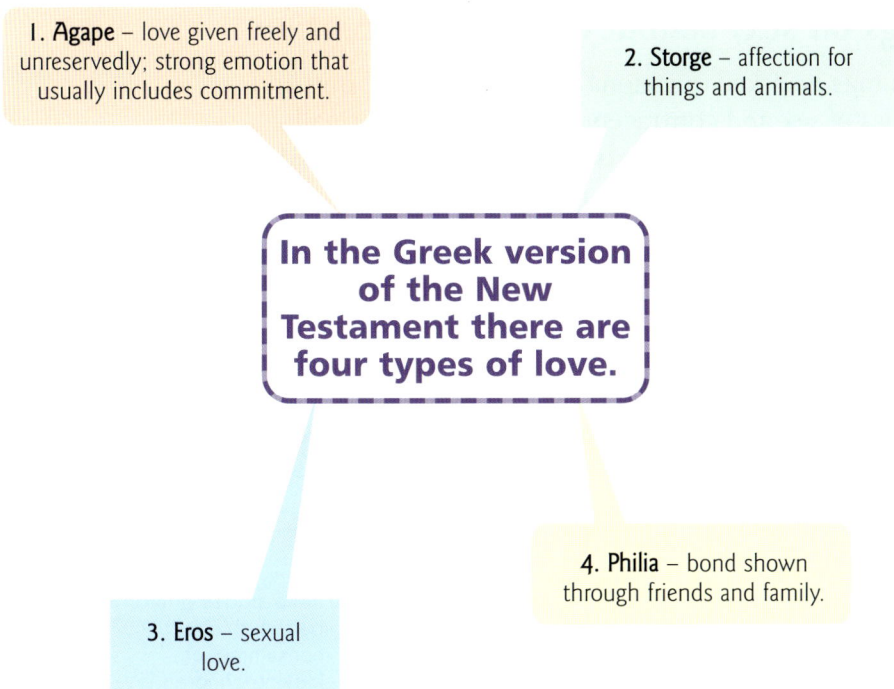

1. **Agape** – love given freely and unreservedly; strong emotion that usually includes commitment.

2. **Storge** – affection for things and animals.

In the Greek version of the New Testament there are four types of love.

4. **Philia** – bond shown through friends and family.

3. **Eros** – sexual love.

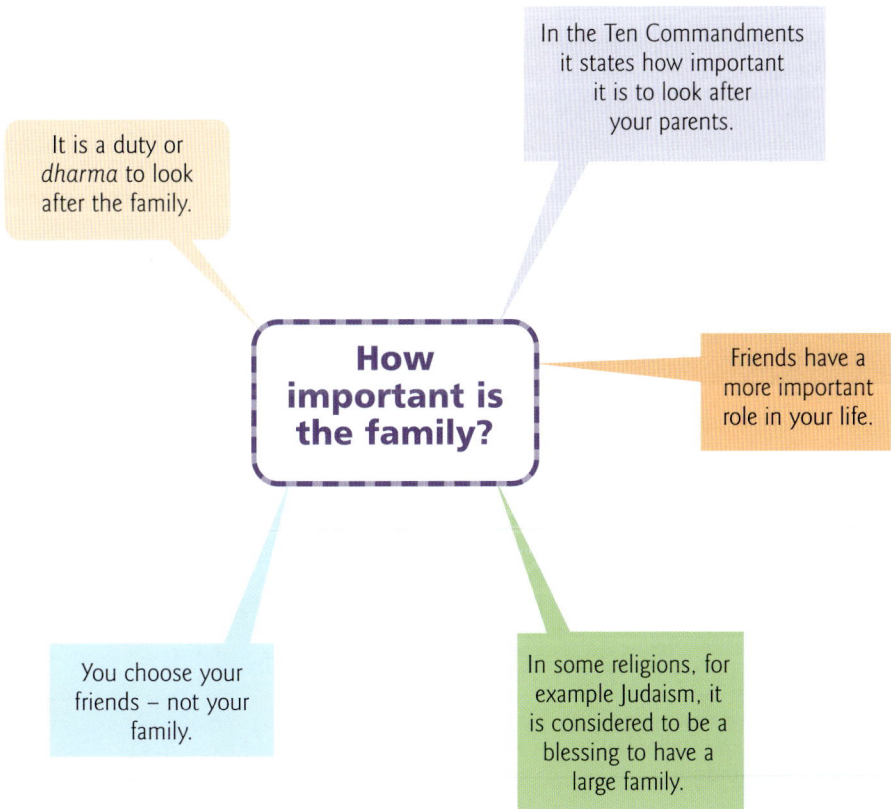

It is a duty or *dharma* to look after the family.

In the Ten Commandments it states how important it is to look after your parents.

How important is the family?

Friends have a more important role in your life.

You choose your friends – not your family.

In some religions, for example Judaism, it is considered to be a blessing to have a large family.

Issues of sex

Religious teachings on sex, celibacy and contraception

In the examination, you may be asked questions on religious teachings and attitudes concerning issues of sex and contraception. These are normally b) and d) questions. You need to answer from two different religious traditions. The key religious teachings are shown below. It is important to remember that there will be different views and practices between believers in the same tradition. Many religions agree on the teachings shown in the 'general' box below.

Key religious teachings: sex, celibacy and contraception

GENERAL
- Sex begins a special committment.
- Sex should take place within a committed relationship such as marriage.
- Sex is holy and sacred.
- Casual sex is seen as devaluing people.
- Adultery is harmful to the special relationship of marriage.

CHRISTIANITY ✚
- Sex is a gift from God.
- Contraceptives are acceptable to many Christians so long as both partners agree.
- Adultery is forbidden in the Ten Commandments.

Roman Catholic churches
- Priests are expected to be celibate.
- Artificial methods of contraception aren't allowed.
- Sex should always allow the possibility of new life.
- Natural methods of contraception are allowed, for example natural family planning.

BUDDHISM ✡
- Buddhist monks and nuns should be celibate to channel energies into religious work.
- Sex must be controlled and not in excess.
- Sex must not cause suffering.
- Buddhists should consider their intentions for using contraceptives and if it goes against the five precepts by causing harm.
- Adultery causes *dukkha* (suffering) and so should be avoided.

HINDUISM ॐ
- Chastity is a *dharma* (duty) of the student stage.
- Sex should only happen within marriage.
- *Kama* (sensual pleasure) is one of the four aims of life.
- Contraception could be against *ahimsa* (non-violence).
- Some perform *garbhadan samskara* to purify the womb.
- A promise of faithfulness is made in the wedding ceremony.
- Faithfulness is shown by the role models of Rama and Sita.

ISLAM ☪
- Sex should only happen within marriage.
- Sex is considered as an act of worship.
- The Pill and condoms are considered more acceptable forms of contraception than those that are difficult to reverse such as a vasectomy.
- Promises of faithfulness are usually made in the wedding ceremony.
- The Qur'an says 'Have nothing to do with adultery.'

JUDAISM ✡
- Sex is seen as one of the three stages of marriage – betrothal/contract/consummation.
- Having children is believed to be part of God's will.
- Condoms where the male seed is destroyed are generally disapproved of.
- The Ten Commandments forbid adultery.
- The Halakhah emphasises that a husband should be sexually considerate.

SIKHISM ☬
- Wearing of *kachs* is a reminder of the need for chastity and faithfulness in a marriage.
- Lust is one of the five evil passions.
- Having children is believed to be part of God's will.
- The *izzat* or honour of a Sikh family is very important.
- The Guru Granth Sahib states 'Do not cast your eyes on the beauty of another's wife'.

Evaluation questions on sex, celibacy and contraception

There are two issues you should be able to evaluate. These are shown in the diagrams below and are often asked in c) and e) types of questions. Around the two issues in the diagrams below are some views (both religious and non-religious) you could include in your answers.

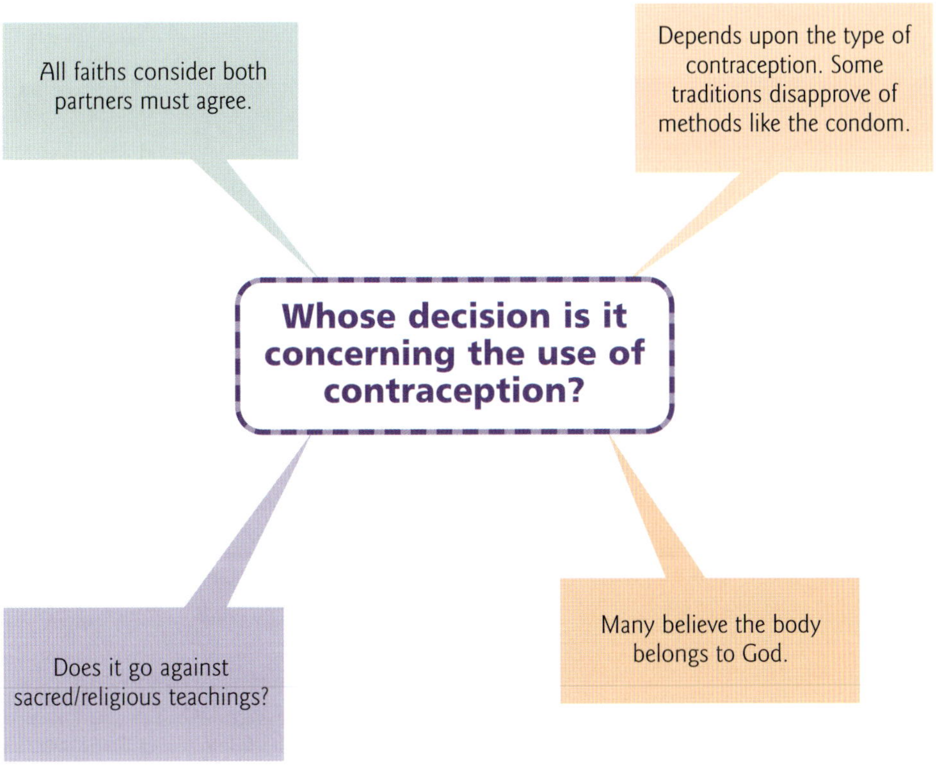

All faiths consider both partners must agree.

Depends upon the type of contraception. Some traditions disapprove of methods like the condom.

Whose decision is it concerning the use of contraception?

Does it go against sacred/religious teachings?

Many believe the body belongs to God.

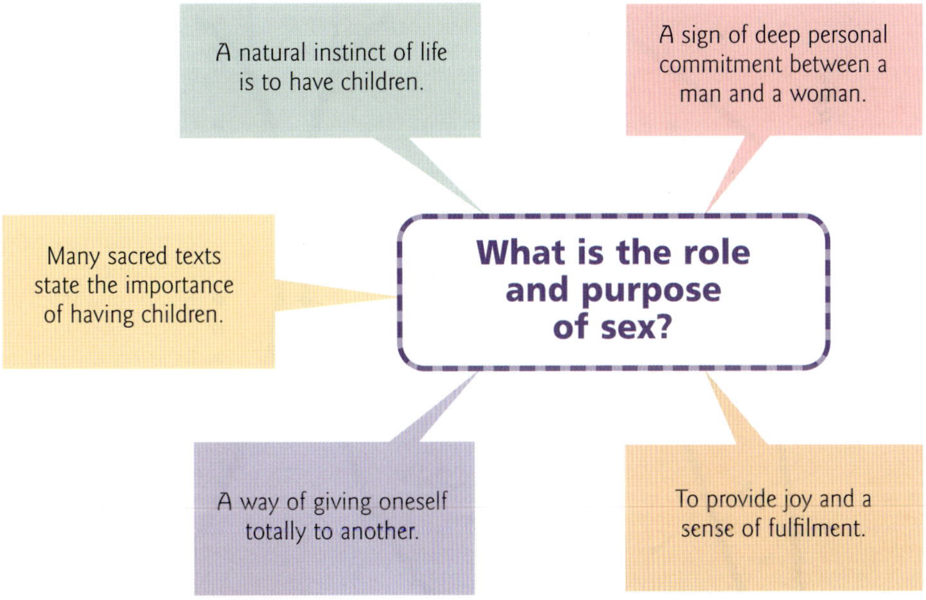

A natural instinct of life is to have children.

A sign of deep personal commitment between a man and a woman.

Many sacred texts state the importance of having children.

What is the role and purpose of sex?

A way of giving oneself totally to another.

To provide joy and a sense of fulfilment.

Exam Tip

This is a Religious Studies examination and in each question you are expected to show the impact that having a religious belief has on the way that believers respond to moral issues.

9

Exam Tip

To gain full marks in evaluation e) questions you should include a range of moral and religious teachings in your arguments and include religious and general specialist language. Look at the points in each of the hands in answer to the question above and use them to help you to answer the question. Work out what specific religious terms from two different religious traditions you could add.

Exam Tip

In your answers it is always a good idea to use relevant material and teachings from other topics.

On the one hand …

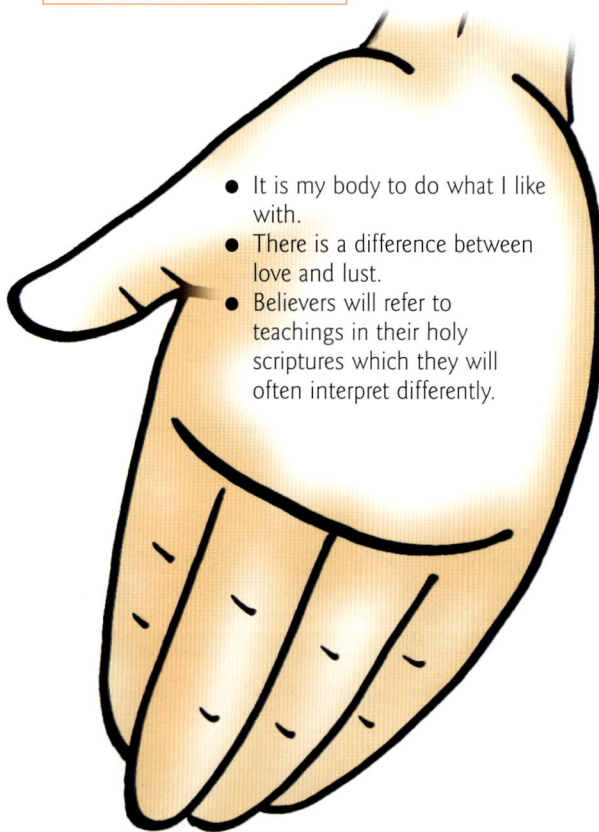

On the other hand …

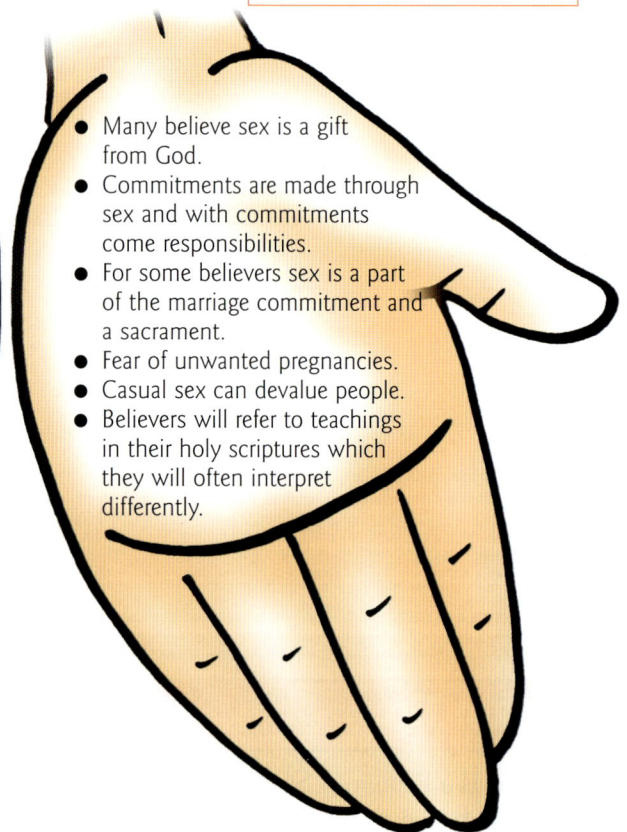

- It is my body to do what I like with.
- There is a difference between love and lust.
- Believers will refer to teachings in their holy scriptures which they will often interpret differently.

- Many believe sex is a gift from God.
- Commitments are made through sex and with commitments come responsibilities.
- For some believers sex is a part of the marriage commitment and a sacrament.
- Fear of unwanted pregnancies.
- Casual sex can devalue people.
- Believers will refer to teachings in their holy scriptures which they will often interpret differently.

Issues of marriage, cohabitation and same-sex relationships

Religious teachings on marriage, cohabitation and same-sex relationships

In the examination, you may be asked questions on religious teachings and attitudes concerning issues of marriage, cohabitation and same-sex relationships. These are normally b) and d) questions. You need to answer from two different religious traditions. The key religious teachings are shown below. It is important to remember that there will be different views and practices between believers in the same tradition. Many religions agree on teachings shown in the 'general' box below.

Key religious teachings: marriage, cohabitation and same-sex relationships

GENERAL
- Marriage is considered important in all religious traditions.
- There is a diversity of customs which will often reflect the country the wedding is taking place in.
- When civil partnerships are blessed in some places of worship, the ceremony is different from the marriage ceremony.

CHRISTIANITY ✝
- Most denominations don't have a betrothal ceremony.
- Marriage is a sacrament within certain denominations such as Roman Catholicism.
- Different attitudes to same-sex marriages:
  - Anglican Church may bless the same-sex couple.
  - Quakers have welcomed same-sex marriages for many years
  - Catholics teach marriage is a union between a woman and a man

BUDDHISM ☸
- No official view on same sex marriages.
- Sex must be controlled within marriage so that no one suffers.

HINDUISM ॐ
- Courtship follows the intention to marry:
  - families of the couple meet
  - couple will have supervised meetings
  - priest will look at horoscopes.
- Wedding is a *samskara*.
- No official view on same-sex marriage; it depends on interpretation of scriptures.

ISLAM ☪
- Many preparations before marriage:
  - families often help to find the right partner.
  - often courtship happens before the wedding.
  - couple's families meet.
  - supervised meetings of the couple.
  - dowry (*mahr*) is arranged.
- Ceremony (*Nikkah*) may take place in a mosque or home.
- Same-sex marriages not allowed.

JUDAISM ✡
- No specific courtship ceremonies.
- Preparation before may include lessons with the rabbi and fasting.
- Liberal Jews often support same-sex marriages.
- Orthodox Jews do not allow same-sex marriages.

SIKHISM ☬
- Role of marriage is to bring two souls together.
- Courtship follows intention to marry.
- Families of the couple will meet.
- It is expected children will be a result of marriage.
- No mention of same-sex marriages in the Guru Granth Sahib.

Religious marriage ceremonies

In the examination, you will need to answer from two different traditions. It is important to remember that there will be different views and practices between believers in the same tradition. Many religions agree on the practices that are shown in the 'general' box below.

Exam Tip

For d) questions you will often be asked to explain the main practices or teachings. Take care to not just describe but to show the importance or reason.

Key religious teachings: key features of religious wedding ceremonies

GENERAL
- Religious weddings are conducted by someone of authority within that tradition, e.g. rabbi, vicar, priest, etc.
- Will often follow the customs of the country.
- Usually held in front of family and friends to show the importance.

CHRISTIANITY ✝
- Often held in a church, chapel or cathedral as this is considered as God's house.
- Purpose of marriage is stated at the start of the service.
- Vows are taken to show commitment, e.g. 'in sickness and in health'.
- Exchange of rings to represent love.
- Sermon or talk about the importance of marriage.
- Singing of hymns to worship God.
- Signing the register to show the couple are married.

Orthodox churches
- Coronation signifies the marriage.
- Couple will drink three times from the same cup symbolising their life together.

Roman Catholic churches
- Everyone present is considered as a witness.
- Wedding takes place sometimes during the Nuptial Mass – showing sacramental nature.

HINDUISM ॐ
- Wedding is a *samskara*.
- *Mandap* (canopy) will be put up in the wedding hall.
- Offerings are made to Ganesha as he is believed to remove obstacles.
- The bride's scarf is tied to the groom's and they circle the *havan* to show togetherness.
- Seven steps are taken for food, strength, wealth, happiness, children, long wedded life and unity.
- The *havan* is lit and offerings made to symbolise wish for fertility, health and prosperity.

ISLAM ☪
- Ceremony includes recitation from the sacred text the Qur'an.
- Agreement to the contract (*mahr*) will be made in front of witnesses.
- Exchange of vows is sometimes made.
- Contract is signed.

JUDAISM
- Often held in a synagogue.
- Held under a *chuppah* as it is often believed that it shows the new home or a sign of God's blessing.
- Blessings of wine to symbolise joy and marriage.
- Signing of the *ketubah* (contract).
- Breaking of a glass to represent the fragility of marriage and also the destruction of the Temple.

SIKHISM ☬
- *Anand Karaj* (marriage service) takes place in front of the Guru Granth Sahib.
- Bride holds the end of husband's scarf to symbolise being joined together.
- Couple walk round the Guru Granth Sahib four times.

BUDDHISM ☸
- Usually the *sangha* chants texts of blessings.
- Sometimes vows stating responsibilities are said.

Evaluation questions on marriage, cohabitation and same-sex relationships

There are three issues you should be able to evaluate. These are shown in the diagrams below and are often asked in c) and e) types of questions. Around the three issues in the diagrams below are some views (both religious and non-religious) you could include in your answers.

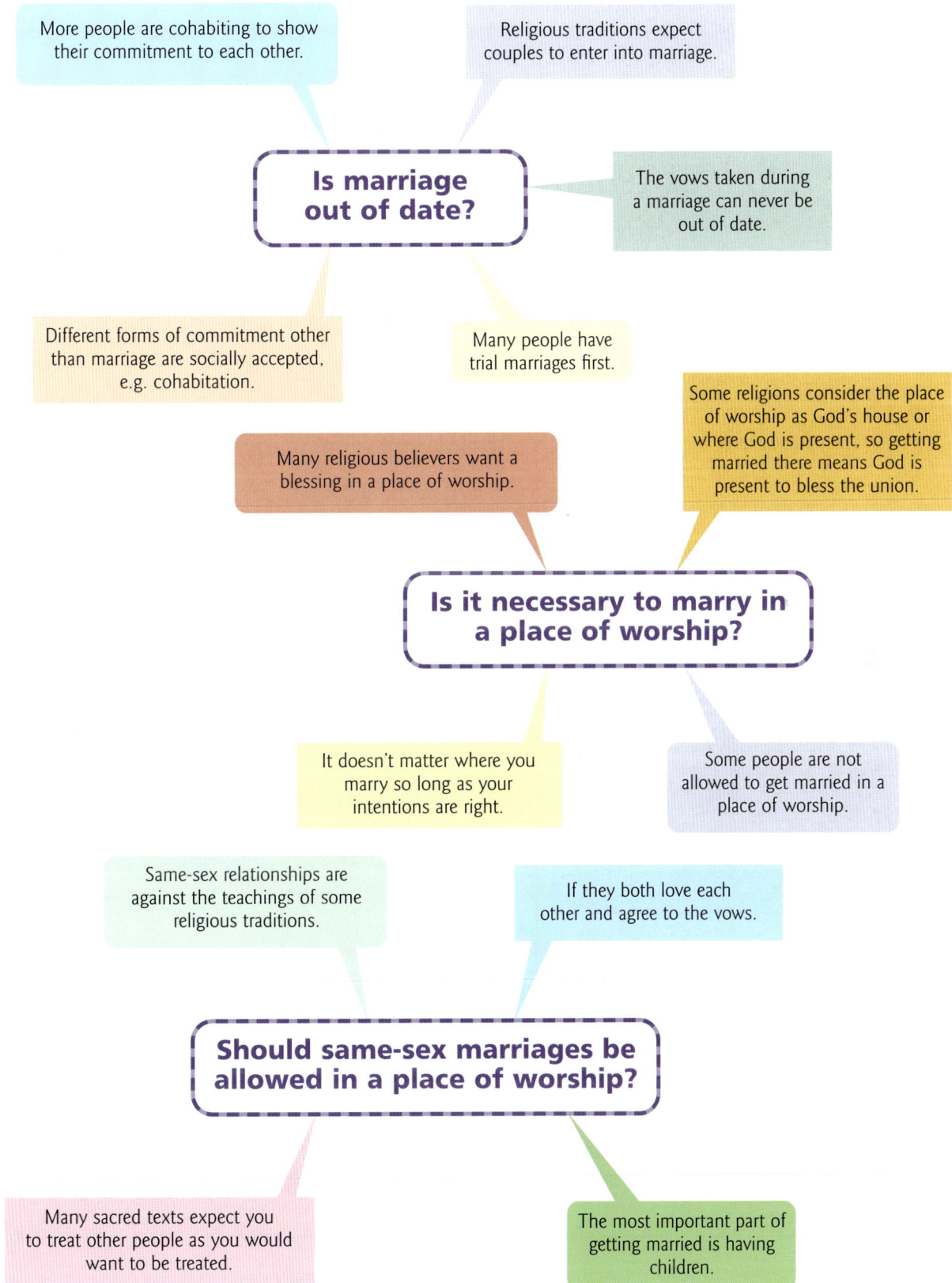

More people are cohabiting to show their commitment to each other.

Religious traditions expect couples to enter into marriage.

Is marriage out of date?

The vows taken during a marriage can never be out of date.

Different forms of commitment other than marriage are socially accepted, e.g. cohabitation.

Many people have trial marriages first.

Some religions consider the place of worship as God's house or where God is present, so getting married there means God is present to bless the union.

Many religious believers want a blessing in a place of worship.

Is it necessary to marry in a place of worship?

It doesn't matter where you marry so long as your intentions are right.

Some people are not allowed to get married in a place of worship.

Same-sex relationships are against the teachings of some religious traditions.

If they both love each other and agree to the vows.

Should same-sex marriages be allowed in a place of worship?

Many sacred texts expect you to treat other people as you would want to be treated.

The most important part of getting married is having children.

13

Issues of divorce and remarriage

Religious teachings on divorce and remarriage

In the examination, you may be asked questions on religious teachings and attitudes concerning issues of divorce and remarriage. These are normally b) and d) questions. You need to answer from two different religious traditions. The key religious teachings are shown below. It is important to remember that there will be different views and practices between believers in the same tradition. Many religions agree on the practices that are shown in the 'general' box below.

Key religious teachings: divorce and remarriage

GENERAL
- Divorce is always regrettable.
- Promises or vows have been made and so show a commitment.
- It often depends on the individual situation.
- Faith communities will try to support the couple in practical and spiritual ways.

CHRISTIANITY ✠
Anglicans, Methodists, United Reform churches
- Divorce is accepted.
- Remarriage is discouraged but if chosen, a non-church wedding is preferred.
- No minister can be forced to conduct a remarriage service.

Roman Catholic churches
- Divorce isn't recognised.
- Marriage is a sacrament and cannot be dissolved unless it is annulled.
- Annulment can happen for cases such as where a partner was forced to marry.

BUDDHISM ☸
- Divorce is allowed as a last resort but the divorce must be for the right intention and the least harm caused.
- Couples can remarry but no suffering (*dukkha*) should be caused.

HINDUISM ॐ
- Divorce is allowed as a last resort but is discouraged because of the sacramental value of the marriage.
- Hindus of lower castes have always been allowed divorce and remarriage.
- Extended family would help a couple to reconcile.

ISLAM ☪
- Divorce is allowed as a last resort (Prophet Muhammad said 'Of all the things which have been permitted divorce is the most hated by Allah').
- On three different occasions the husband must state in front of witnesses that the marriage is over.
- The *iddah* period (three months) follows where the couple stay in the same house to support reconciliation.
- Divorce will mean the wife is given the final part of her dowry.
- Remarriage is allowed.

JUDAISM ☰
- Divorcing couples must obtain both a religious and civil divorce.
- Husbands in Orthodox Judaism must give their wife a *get* (document of divorce).
- Remarriage can happen 90 days after the receiving of the *get*.
- Some men refuse to give their wives a divorce (*agunot*).

SIKHISM ☬
- Marriage is a union of two souls but divorce is sometimes necessary.
- Families will often try to help a couple remarry.
- Remarriages can take place in a place of worship.

Evaluation questions on divorce and remarriage

There are three issues you should be able to evaluate. These are shown in the diagrams below and are often asked in c) and e) types of questions. Around the three issues in the diagrams below are some views (both religious and non-religious) you could include in your answers.

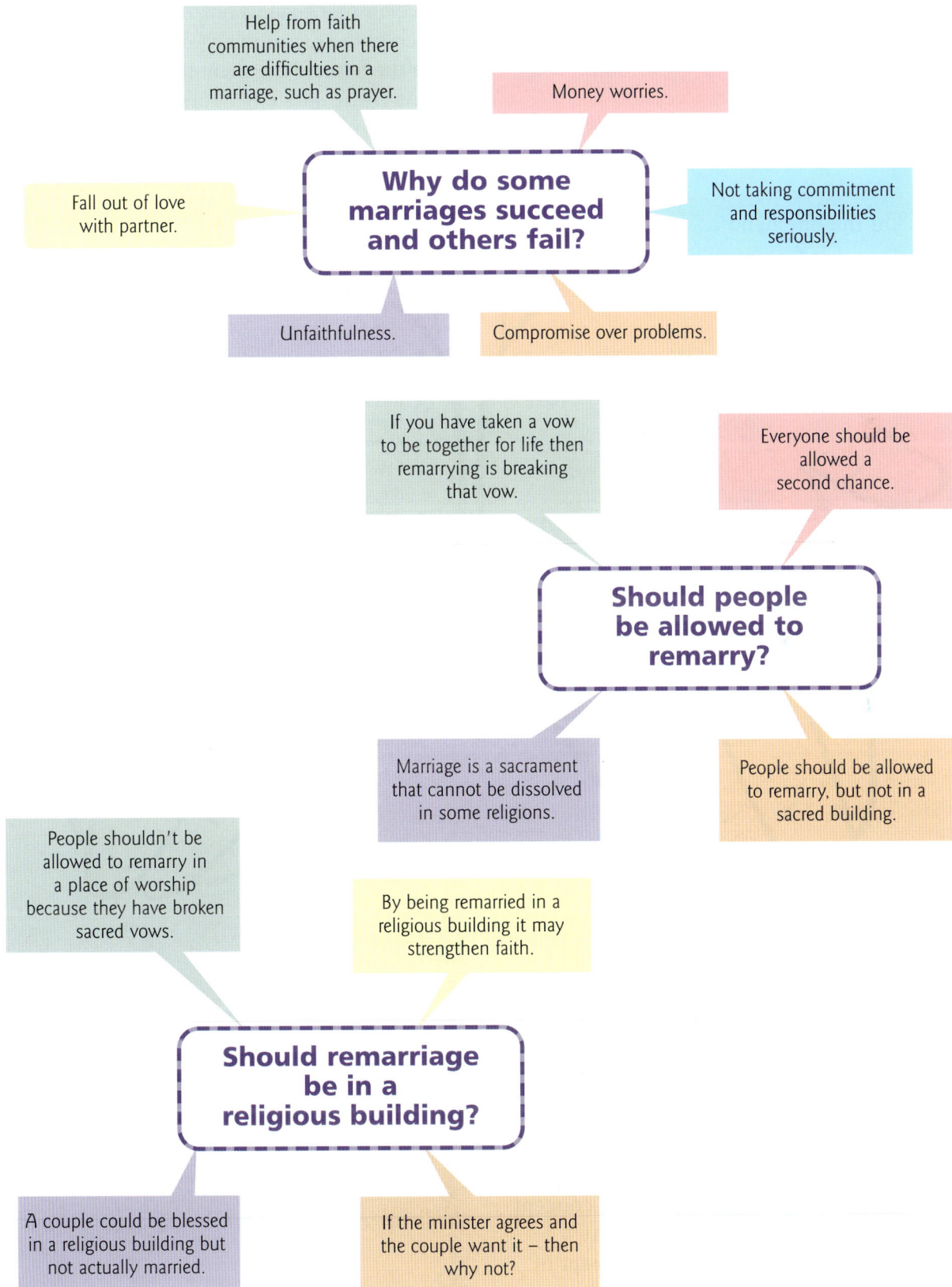

Help from faith communities when there are difficulties in a marriage, such as prayer.

Money worries.

Fall out of love with partner.

Why do some marriages succeed and others fail?

Not taking commitment and responsibilities seriously.

Unfaithfulness.

Compromise over problems.

If you have taken a vow to be together for life then remarrying is breaking that vow.

Everyone should be allowed a second chance.

Should people be allowed to remarry?

Marriage is a sacrament that cannot be dissolved in some religions.

People should be allowed to remarry, but not in a sacred building.

People shouldn't be allowed to remarry in a place of worship because they have broken sacred vows.

By being remarried in a religious building it may strengthen faith.

Should remarriage be in a religious building?

A couple could be blessed in a religious building but not actually married.

If the minister agrees and the couple want it – then why not?

15

Exam Tip

To gain full marks in evaluation e) questions you should include a range of moral and religious teachings in your arguments and include religious and general specialist language. Look at the points in each of the hands in answer to the question on the left and use them to help you to answer the question. Work out what specific religious terms from two different religious traditions you could add.

On the one hand …

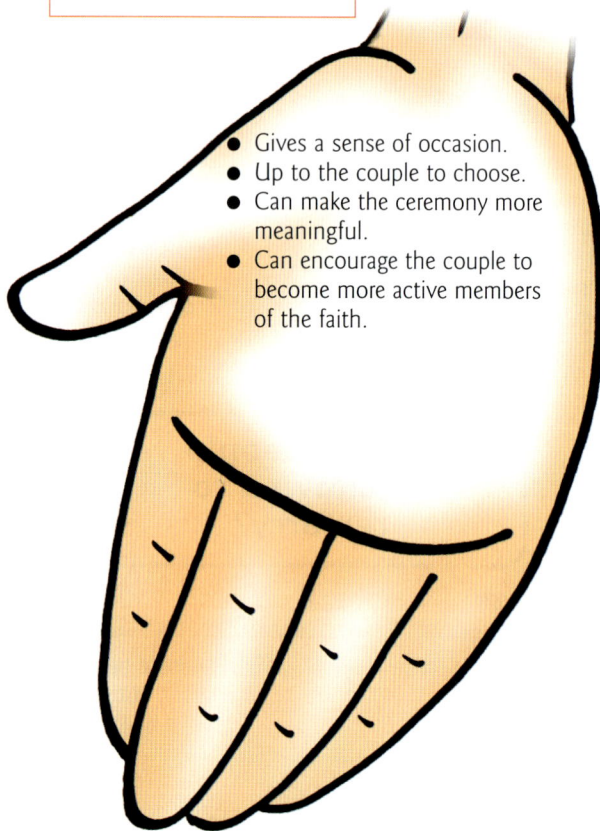

On the other hand …

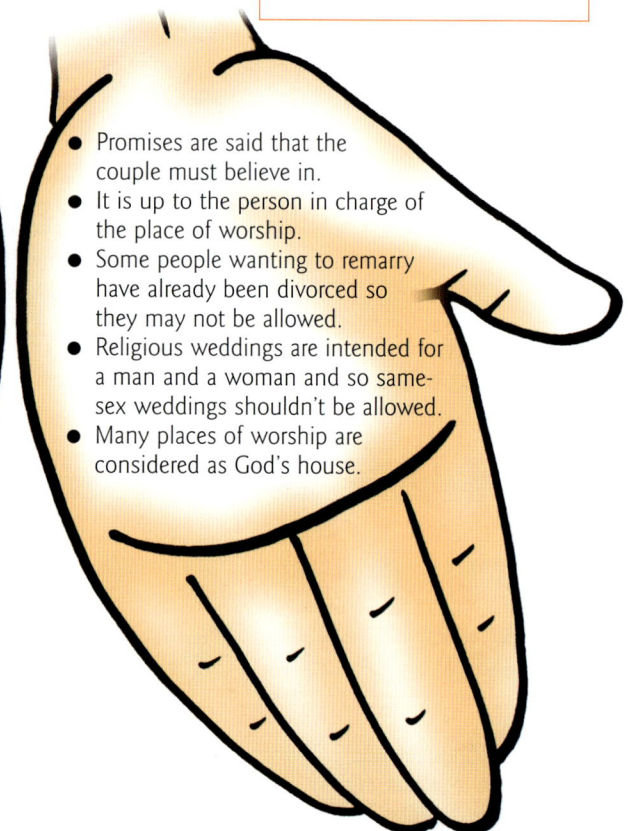

- Gives a sense of occasion.
- Up to the couple to choose.
- Can make the ceremony more meaningful.
- Can encourage the couple to become more active members of the faith.

- Promises are said that the couple must believe in.
- It is up to the person in charge of the place of worship.
- Some people wanting to remarry have already been divorced so they may not be allowed.
- Religious weddings are intended for a man and a woman and so same-sex weddings shouldn't be allowed.
- Many places of worship are considered as God's house.

Activity

All marriages have ups and downs. Some differences are easily reconciled while others can result in conflict and divorce.

Look back at all you have learnt so far. Now copy out and complete the two acrostics opposite, one for why marriages succeed using the key concept of reconciliation, and one for why marriages fail using the key concept of conflict.

R
Eros
Commitment
O
N
C
I
L
I
A
Talking about problems
I
O
N

C
O
N
F
Lust
I
C
T

EXAMINATION PRACTICE

It is important that you understand the structure of the examination paper. This is explained in the Introduction on page 2.

Below are practice questions for each question type in the examination. After each of the questions there is a specimen answer which has been given a mark. Look at the levels of response grids on pages 67–8 and try to improve each answer to get full marks.

Question a) Explain what religious believers mean by love. (2 marks)

Answer When you care for someone.   (Level 1 = 1 mark)

Question b) Explain how religious believers might help others with marriage difficulties? (4 marks)

Answer They might help by shopping for them and looking after the children.
(Level 1 = 1 mark)

Question c) 'Sex before marriage harms no one.' Give two reasons why a religious believer might agree or disagree with this statement. (4 marks)

Answer Many Christians may disagree as sex is considered to be a gift from God and therefore should only take place within marriage.   (Level 2 = 2 marks)

Question d) Explain from two different religious traditions the attitude towards divorce (6 marks)

Answer Christians don't like divorce because it goes against the Bible and the teachings of Jesus. Muslims don't like divorce but allow it. They will try to help to keep the couple together.   (Level 3 = 3 marks)

Question e) 'Same-sex marriages should be allowed in a place of worship.' Do you agree? Give reasons or evidence for your answer showing that you have thought about more than one point of view. You must include references to religious beliefs in your answer. (8 marks)

Answer They should because then the couple can be happy and it is their human right. On the other hand they shouldn't because marriages are expected to take place between a man and a woman. They could have a blessing though in a place of worship if they felt that it was important for them.   (Level 2 = 4 marks)

Topic 2 Is it fair?

The Big Picture

Below is a summary of the key concepts, religious teachings and human experiences you need to know for the examination.

You need to know these!
The a) questions in the examination will ask you about these key concepts, *and* you should also use them in other questions as well.

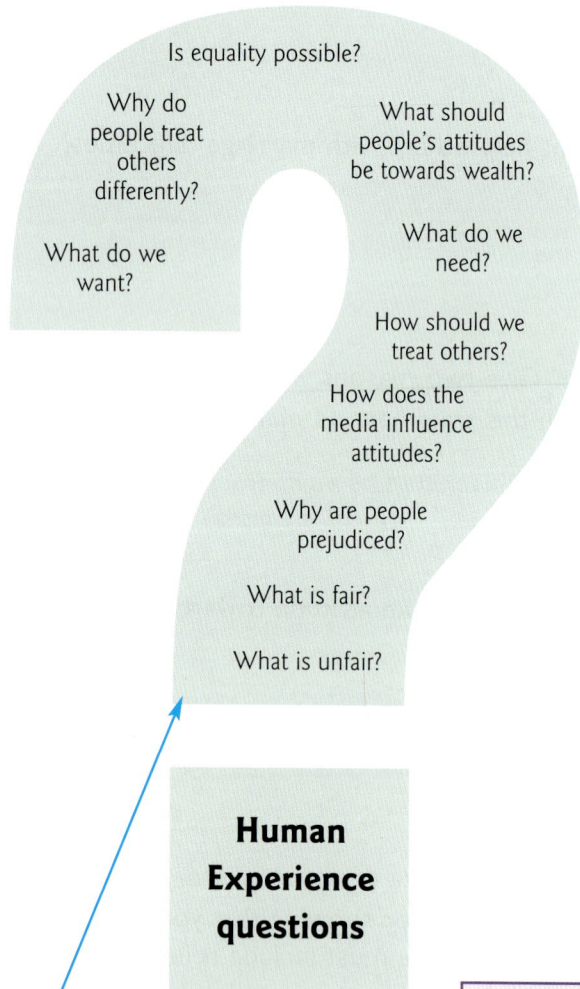

Is equality possible?

Why do people treat others differently?

What should people's attitudes be towards wealth?

What do we want?

What do we need?

How should we treat others?

How does the media influence attitudes?

Why are people prejudiced?

What is fair?

What is unfair?

Human Experience questions

Key concepts to think about ▼

AUTHORITY

DISCRIMINATION

EQUALITY

IDENTITY

INJUSTICE

PREJUDICE

Questions like these will be asked in c) and e) questions in the examination.

The religious teachings here *should* be used in b), c), d), and e) questions. You need to know religious teachings for two traditions.

Religious teachings to explore
- Human dignity
- Equality
- Use of wealth
  - Charity
- Social responsibility
  - Religion and the media
- Religious commitments to promote justice
- Racial, social and gender divisions
- People and organisations who have worked for justice
- Religious responses to injustice

Religious and specialist terms

On the screen below are some religious and specialist terms you could use throughout the topic. You should be able to use terms from two different religious traditions or two denominations of Christianity. Definitions can be found in the Glossary on pages 69–70.

General specialist terms
campaign, civil disobedience, dignity, equal opportunities, evangelise, the 'Golden Rule', human rights, influence, justice, materialism, media, ordained, pray, prejudge, sacred texts, spiritual values, vocation

Christian terms
Bible, Image of God, Jesus, Parable of the Good Samaritan, Zaccheus

Buddhist terms
the Buddha, enlightenment, illusory, *metta*, Middle Way

Hindu terms
ahimsa, atman, artha, dharma, puja

Muslim terms
five pillars, *haram*, imam, Prophet Muhammad, *sadaqah, ummah, zakah*

Jewish terms
mitzvah, rabbi, *Shabbat*, synagogue, *Tzedaka*

Sikh terms
Gurdwara, Guru Granth Sahib, *langar, seva*, Five Ks

Exam Tip

It is important to use general specialist terms and terms from the religions you have studied in your answers to examination questions.

Exam Tip

If you can use stories or teachings from sacred texts to support your answer it will help you get high marks. You don't need to remember the exact words. You can make general references or put them in your own words.

19

Key concepts

There are six key concepts in this topic. The definition of each is shown in the keys below. The first examination question for each topic (question a)) will ask you to explain one of the key concepts for two marks. You should also refer to the key concepts in answers to other examination questions on the topic.

Authority
Right or power over others. It may be a person such as a priest, a set of laws, or the teachings from a sacred text.

Discrimination
Treating people differently because of their race, gender, religion or class. Religious believers would say it is wrong as everyone is part of a divine creation.

Equality
Being treated the same. Many religious believers would say all people are equal in God's eyes.

Identity
The personality and character of an individual. Each person has their own identity and is unique.

Injustice
Withholding someone's human rights, for example, imprisonment without trial.

Prejudice
When a person is judged without any evidence. All religious traditions agree that people should treat others as they wish to be treated.

Issues to consider

There are four main areas you will need to know about for this topic:
- religious teachings on human dignity
- issues of justice, injustice and social responsibility
- issues of equality
- issues of wealth and charity.

Religious teachings on human dignity

Before beginning to think about issues of justice and equality it is important to consider the religious beliefs concerning human dignity. Many religious believers consider it important to treat each other with respect and dignity because all life is sacred (see page 54). This key belief in the dignity and sanctity of all life guides religious believers' practices and beliefs on many issues connected with justice and injustice. Many religions agree on the teachings shown in the 'general' box below.

Key religious teachings: human dignity

GENERAL
- Religious believers are expected to treat all people with dignity.
- Many religious texts state that God made every human being.

CHRISTIANITY ✝
- Christians believe God is the creator of all and believe all people are 'One in Christ' (Galatians 3).
- Jesus showed in his teachings and actions that all people have human dignity.
- Jesus mixed with tax collectors like Zaccheus and showed the importance of caring for all through parables, such as the Parable of the Good Samaritan.
- Christian charities such as the Campaign for Racial Justice (CARJ) encourage racial justice and support refugees and asylum seekers.

BUDDHISM ☸
- Buddhists believe all humans have the possibility of enlightenment so it is important to show compassion and loving kindness (metta) to all.
- Stories from the life of the Buddha show how he tried to treat everyone with dignity. Even outcasts like Angulimala were treated with respect.
- Cakkavatti Sihananada Sutta states, 'Whoever in your kingdom is poor, to him let some help be given'.
- Buddhist charities such as Karuna Trust address the injustices prejudice can cause to others. Karuna means compassionate action based on wisdom.

HINDUISM ॐ
- Hinduism teaches all people contain atman.
- While Hindus are on earth they believe it is important to help others.
- One of the four aims in life is artha – to make wealth to support others.
- Hindu charities such as Food for Life provide free meals for all.

ISLAM ☪
- Muslims believe Allah is the creator of all humans and they must take responsibility for others.
- The community of believers, ummah, are expected to support each other.
- The Prophet Muhammad taught the importance of equal opportunities for women – especially widows.
- The Qur'an teaches it is important to 'free a slave or to give food in the day of hunger'.
- Muslim charities such as Islamic Relief aim to help the poorest people through both long- and short-term aid.
- Men and women are considered equal before Allah and are expected to keep the Five Pillars. Although women can be teachers of religion they cannot become imams.

JUDAISM 🕎
- Jews believe God is the creator of all life. In Leviticus it states, 'When a stranger stays with you in your land, you shall not do him wrong'.
- It is a mitzvah (required act) to treat all with dignity.
- Jewish charities such as Tzedek (justice) aim to eliminate poverty regardless of race and religion.

SIKHISM ☬
- Sikhs believe it is important to offer service (seva) to all and many gurdwaras offer a free langar to all.
- The Guru Granth Sahib states, 'A place in God's court can only be attained if we do service to others in the world'.
- Sikh charities such as Sikhcess base their community action on equality, social justice and service.

Issues of justice, injustice and social responsibility

Seeking justice for others and responding to injustices are important actions in all religious traditions.

Believers take social responsibility and aim to make sure that:

- human rights are observed
- all people have equal opportunities
- all people are treated without discrimination.

There are many ways that individuals may show social responsibility and seek justice for others:

C ivil disobedience, for example when Rosa Parks' actions led to the bus boycott

A lert the media to the injustices, for example publicise campaigns such as Racial Justice Sunday

M ake sermons and speeches in places of worship, such as Martin Luther King Jr

P rotest marches and petitions, such as the Salt March led by Gandhi for Indian independence

A ctivities to raise money for charities, such as Christian Aid and Red Crescent

I nform others through pamphlets and interfaith dialogue

G roup and individual prayer, such as praying for peace

N on violent actions, such as fasting

Exam Tip

In the examination if you are asked for religious responses or attitudes make sure you include specific religious examples or language.

Evaluation questions on justice, injustice and social responsibility

There are four issues you should be able to evaluate. These are shown in the diagrams below and on page 23 and are often asked in c) and e) types of questions. Around the four issues in the diagrams below are some views (both religious and non-religious) you could include in your answers.

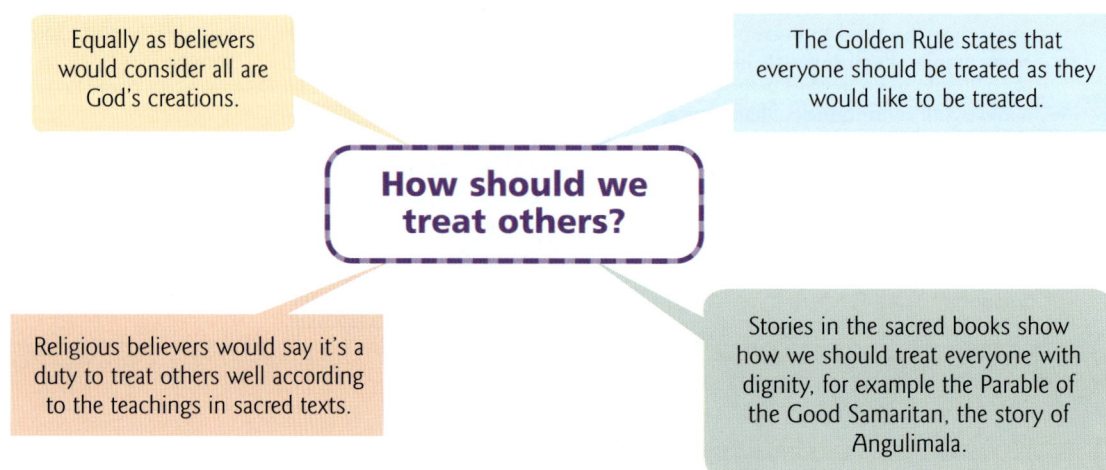

Equally as believers would consider all are God's creations.

The Golden Rule states that everyone should be treated as they would like to be treated.

How should we treat others?

Religious believers would say it's a duty to treat others well according to the teachings in sacred texts.

Stories in the sacred books show how we should treat everyone with dignity, for example the Parable of the Good Samaritan, the story of Angulimala.

When there are equal opportunities.

When there is justice.

What is fair?

When everyone has similar treatment.

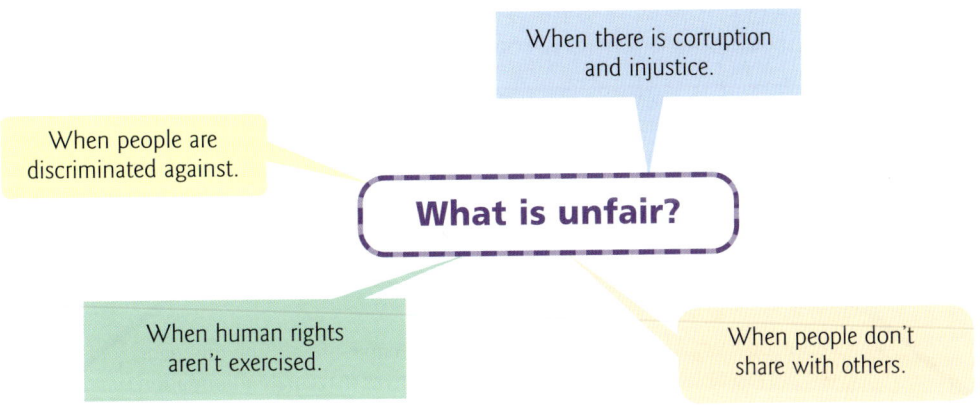

When there is corruption and injustice.

When people are discriminated against.

What is unfair?

When human rights aren't exercised.

When people don't share with others.

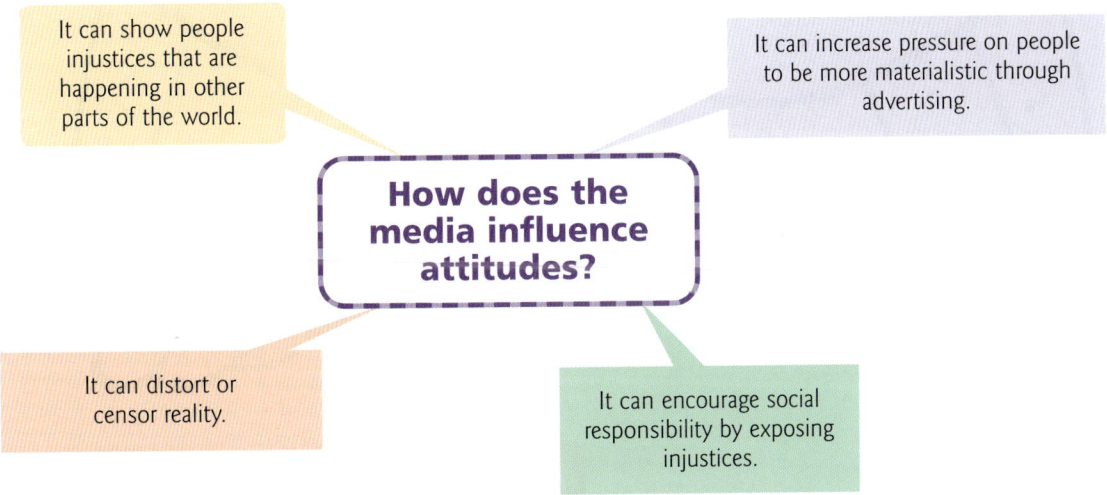

It can show people injustices that are happening in other parts of the world.

It can increase pressure on people to be more materialistic through advertising.

How does the media influence attitudes?

It can distort or censor reality.

It can encourage social responsibility by exposing injustices.

'People's attitudes to social responsibility are never changed by the media.' Do you agree? Give reasons or evidence for your answer showing that you have thought about more than one point of view. You must include references to religious beliefs in your answer.

Exam Tip

To gain full marks in evaluation e) questions you should include a range of moral and religious teachings in your arguments and include religious and general specialist language. Look at the points in each of the hands in answer to the question above and use them to help you to answer the question. Work out what specific religious terms from two different religious traditions you could add.

On the one hand …

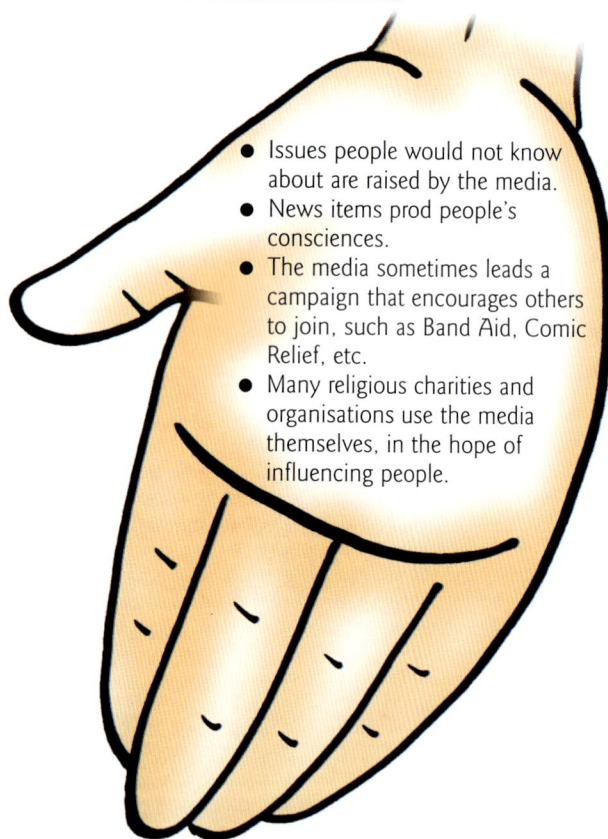

On the other hand …

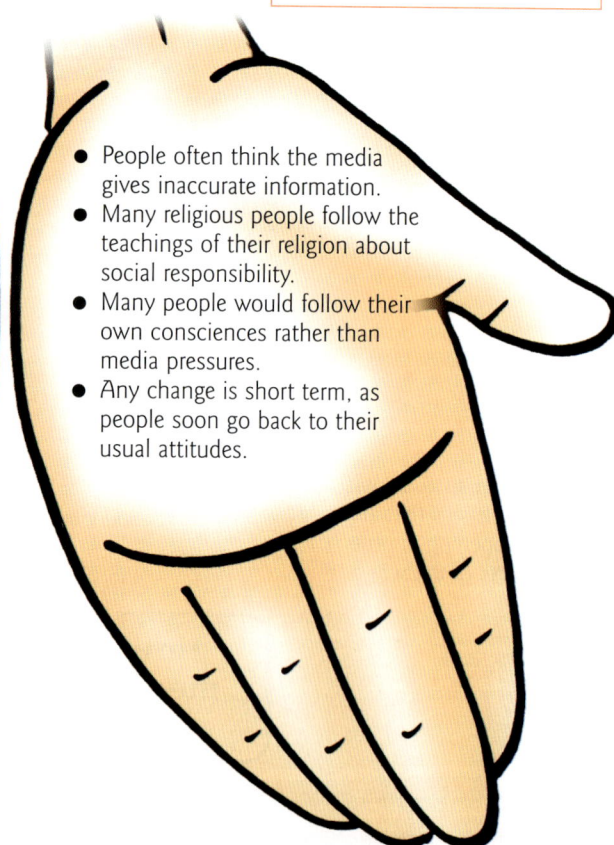

- Issues people would not know about are raised by the media.
- News items prod people's consciences.
- The media sometimes leads a campaign that encourages others to join, such as Band Aid, Comic Relief, etc.
- Many religious charities and organisations use the media themselves, in the hope of influencing people.

- People often think the media gives inaccurate information.
- Many religious people follow the teachings of their religion about social responsibility.
- Many people would follow their own consciences rather than media pressures.
- Any change is short term, as people soon go back to their usual attitudes.

Exam Tip

Many candidates in the examination get prejudice and discrimination confused. Remember, prejudice is the belief or thought, and discrimination is the action.

Issues of equality

Religious teachings on racial, social and gender divisions

In the examination, you may be asked questions on religious teachings concerning racial, social and gender divisions. These are normally b) and d) questions. You need to answer from two different religious traditions. The key religious teachings are outlined below. Many religions agree on the teachings that are shown in the 'general' box below.

Key religious teachings: racial, social and gender divisions

GENERAL
- People should be treated as they would like to be treated themselves (the Golden Rule).
- There is often a difference between religious teachings and the practices that might happen in some cultures or countries.
- Although people are equal that doesn't mean they are all the same. Each person is unique.
- There are different practices and beliefs within each religion.

HINDUISM ॐ
- *Ahimsa* (harmlessness) is a key practice and therefore people shouldn't be hurt because of their race, gender or social status.
- Women have a very important role at home where they perform *puja* (ceremonial worship).

JUDAISM
- As all humanity is made by God, people also have a responsibility to God.
- Israel accepts Jews from all nations and races.
- Women are expected to take an important role in religious ceremonies in the home such as bringing in *Shabbat*.
- In the Orthodox tradition, women are unable to be rabbis and sit separately from men in the synagogue.

ISLAM ☪
- All people are created by Allah.
- The *ummah* (brotherhood) crosses all national, cultural, racial and gender division.
- The act of prayer stresses the importance of equality as worshippers should stand shoulder to shoulder equal before God.
- The Prophet Muhammad showed respect for women and the poor.

CHRISTIANITY ✝
- God created all human beings as equal regardless of gender or race.
- Jesus' example of dealing with lepers and outcasts and his teachings such as the Parable of the Good Samaritan show the importance of caring for all.
- Many Christians such as Martin Luther King Jr and Bishop Tutu have led campaigns against discrimination.
- Although Jesus didn't have any female apostles, much of his teaching and miracles were with women.
- There are different practices depending on denominations as to whether women are allowed to be ordained:
  - In the Methodist and Anglican Church women can be priests and ministers.
  - In the Roman Catholic Church women cannot be ordained as priests or deacons.

SIKHISM ☬
- The Sikh Gurus said that all life belongs to God and that reunion with God is open to all.
- The *langar* shows how everyone is considered equal and welcome to eat together.
- Men and women are allowed to wear the Five Ks.
- To show equal status, men take on the name 'Singh' (lion) and women 'Kaur' (princess).

BUDDHISM ☸
- All people are equal and have within them the possibility of enlightenment.
- *Metta* (loving kindness) should be shown to all.
- Things that separate people, such as wealth, race and power, are all illusory.
- Some Buddhist traditions have nuns although in the Theravada tradition full ordination no longer occurs.

Evaluation questions on equality

There are two issues you should be able to evaluate. These are shown in the diagrams below and are often asked in c) and e) types of questions. Around the two issues in the diagrams below are some views (both religious and non-religious) you could include in your answers.

Exam Tip

Both of these questions ask the *why* not the *how*. Your answers should show the reasons why people are prejudiced and treat others differently.

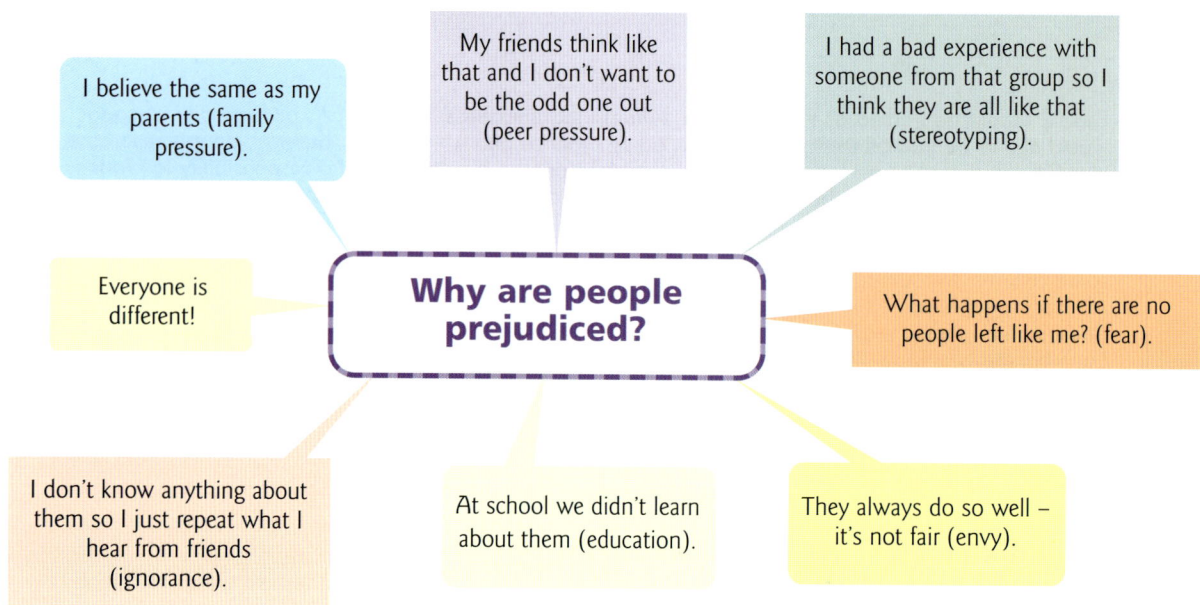

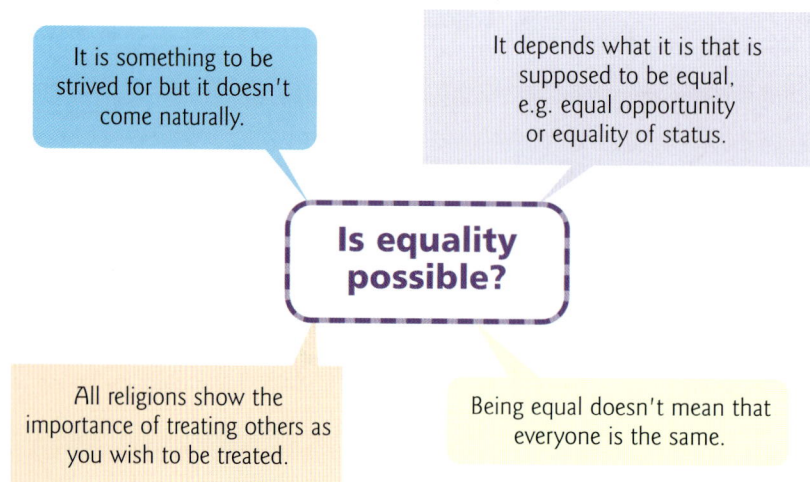

I believe the same as my parents (family pressure).

My friends think like that and I don't want to be the odd one out (peer pressure).

I had a bad experience with someone from that group so I think they are all like that (stereotyping).

Everyone is different!

Why are people prejudiced?

What happens if there are no people left like me? (fear).

I don't know anything about them so I just repeat what I hear from friends (ignorance).

At school we didn't learn about them (education).

They always do so well – it's not fair (envy).

It is something to be strived for but it doesn't come naturally.

It depends what it is that is supposed to be equal, e.g. equal opportunity or equality of status.

Is equality possible?

All religions show the importance of treating others as you wish to be treated.

Being equal doesn't mean that everyone is the same.

Exam Tip

The evaluation questions give you the opportunity to apply all the relevant information you have learnt. Before answering the 8-mark e) questions it is important that you have thought about the evidence you could use. The SWAWOS framework opposite should help you to do this.

SWAWOS framework

S	elect specialist language
W	hat do I think and why?
A	pply religious teaching or example
W	hat's another view?
O	ffer religious teachings
S	uggest impact

Activity

Jayne is about to answer the following examination question:

'There will always be discrimination in society.' Do you agree? Give reasons or evidence for your answer, showing that you have thought about more than one point of view. You must include references to religious beliefs in your answer. (8 *marks*)

She is using the SWAWOS framework to help her frame the key points before answering the question.

Select specialist language

Discrimination, Good Samaritan, Golden Rule, free will, *Shoah*, sanctity of life.

What do I think and why?

Agree because people have free will.

Apply religious teaching or example

People often act as bystanders to injustice despite their religious beliefs, for example, during the Holocaust/Shoah or American Civil Rights.

What's another view?

Many people work to end discrimination/Golden Rule.

Offer religious teachings

Importance of sanctity of life, parable of the Good Samaritan.

Suggest impact

Religious teachings encourage believers to campaign against discrimination in many different forms and not to give up.

Now write an answer to the question, either using Jayne's key points or applying your own to the SWAWOS framework.

Issues of wealth and charity

Religious teachings on wealth and charity

In the examination, you may be asked questions on religious teachings and attitudes concerning issues of wealth and charity. These are normally b) and d) questions. You need to answer from two different religious traditions. The key religious teachings are outlined below. It is important to remember that there will be different views and practices between believers in the same tradition. Many religions agree on the teachings that are shown in the 'general' box below.

Key religious teachings: wealth and charity

GENERAL
- Material wealth isn't the most important thing in life.
- Your afterlife is not dependent on your amount of wealth at death
- It is important how you use your wealth.
- Money should be earned honestly.
- Spiritual values are more important.
- All have charities to help others.

CHRISTIANITY ✝
- Jesus taught 'Blessed are you who are poor, yours is the kingdom of God'.
- The Bible teaches the importance of sharing, e.g. John the Baptist taught that those with two coats must share one.
- Many Christians will try to work in vocational jobs where they are helping others.
- Giving to charity has always been important and some Christians tithe/give a regular amount to charity.
- Some Christian denominations such as The Religious Society of Friends (Quakers) and Methodists do not take part in gambling nor the lottery.
- The Bible states: 'The love of money is the root of all evil'.

HINDUISM ॐ
- Wealth is loaned by God and therefore it is important how it is used.
- Personal wealth should be gained through lawful means (artha).
- Material possessions aren't of lasting value.
- 'What's called worldly possessions is impermanent for by things unstable, the stable cannot be obtained.' (Katha' Upanishad).

ISLAM ☪
- Wealth is a gift from Allah and so should be cared for.
- It is a duty to help others.
- Paying zakah (over two per cent of income) is one of the Five Pillars.
- Voluntary payments (sadaqah) and voluntary work are encouraged.
- Occupations involving gambling, pornography or alcohol are haram – no Muslim should work in them.
- Money should not be gained or lost through gambling.

JUDAISM ✡
- All possessions belong to God.
- Proverbs teaches: 'Don't wear yourself out trying to get rich. Be wise enough to control yourself. Wealth can vanish in the wink of an eye'.
- No money should be used on Shabbat.
- Many Jews give money to charity but not boasting about it is important.
- Families often use pushkes or collecting boxes.
- It is considered a mitzvah (duty) to care and support others.

SIKHISM ☬
- Money shouldn't be spent or gained through gambling or alcohol.
- Many Sikhs give one tenth of their wealth to those in need.
- Seva (service) is an important principle in Sikhism.

BUDDHISM ☸
- The Buddha gave up a life of riches and he taught that craving for materialism leads to suffering.
- The middle way is the aim of life, not to have too much or too little.
- It is important to gain money honestly.
- The Friends of the Western Buddhist Order have many shops and cafés that trade according to Buddhist principles and teachings.
- Helping others is one of the most important Buddhist virtues: 'Whoever in your kingdom is poor, to him let some help be given' (Cakkavatti Sihananda Sutta).

Evaluation questions on wealth and charity

There are two issues you should be able to evaluate. These are shown in the diagrams below and are often asked in c) and e) types of questions. Around the two issues in the diagrams below are some views (both religious and non-religious) you could include in your answers.

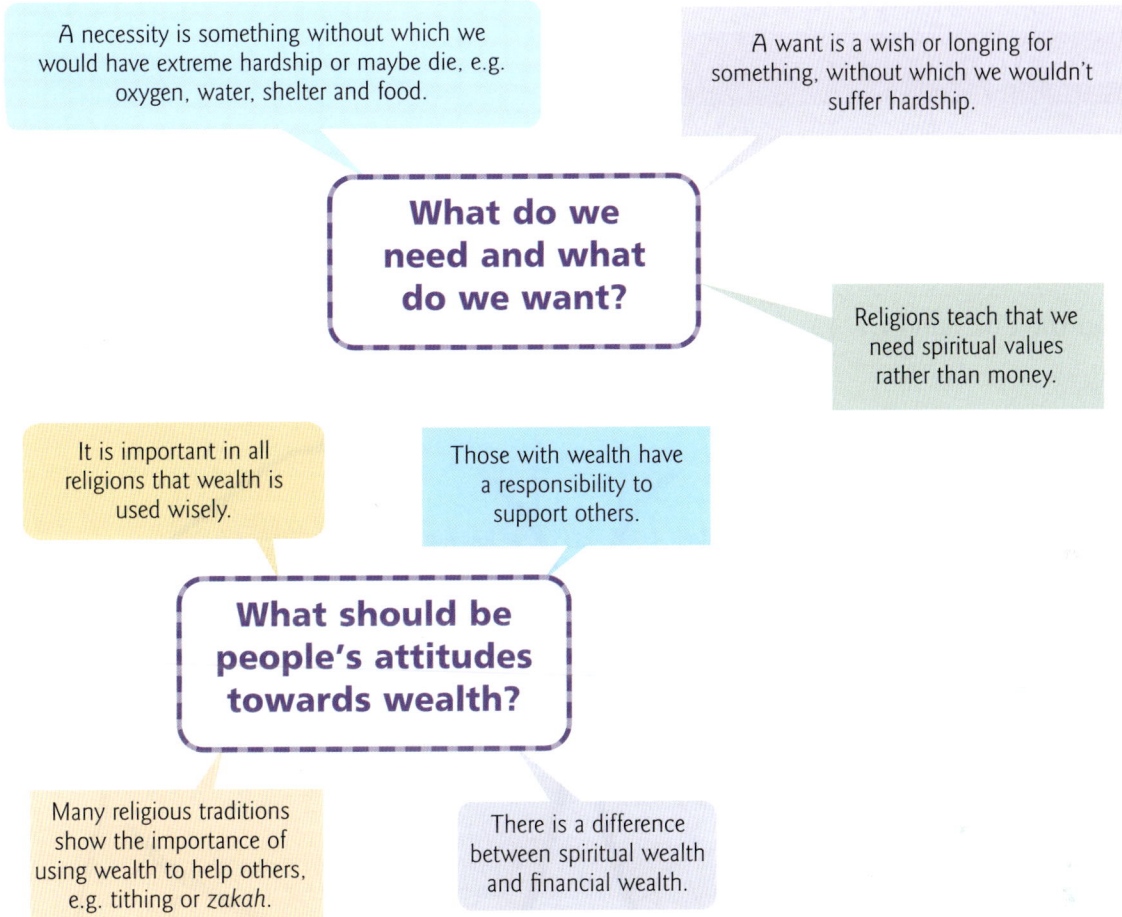

A necessity is something without which we would have extreme hardship or maybe die, e.g. oxygen, water, shelter and food.

A want is a wish or longing for something, without which we wouldn't suffer hardship.

What do we need and what do we want?

Religions teach that we need spiritual values rather than money.

It is important in all religions that wealth is used wisely.

Those with wealth have a responsibility to support others.

What should be people's attitudes towards wealth?

Many religious traditions show the importance of using wealth to help others, e.g. tithing or *zakah*.

There is a difference between spiritual wealth and financial wealth.

Activity

From the list below decide which are our needs and wants:

- games console
- plasma TV
- mobile phone
- oxygen
- medicines
- water
- a home
- friends
- food
- a computer

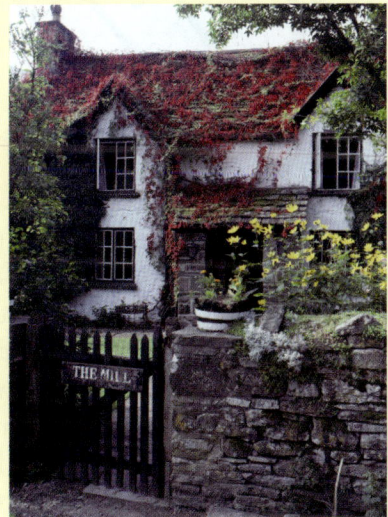

Q 'Wealth should be used for oneself first.' Do you agree? Give reasons or evidence for your answer, showing that you have thought about more than one point of view. You must include references to religious beliefs in your answers.

Exam Tip

In your answers it is always good to use relevant material and teachings from other topics.

On the one hand ...

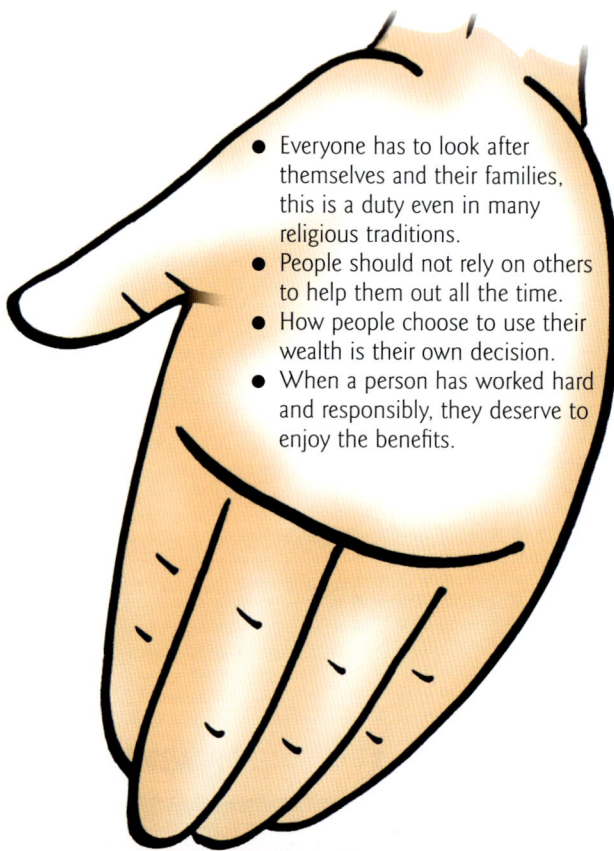

On the other hand ...

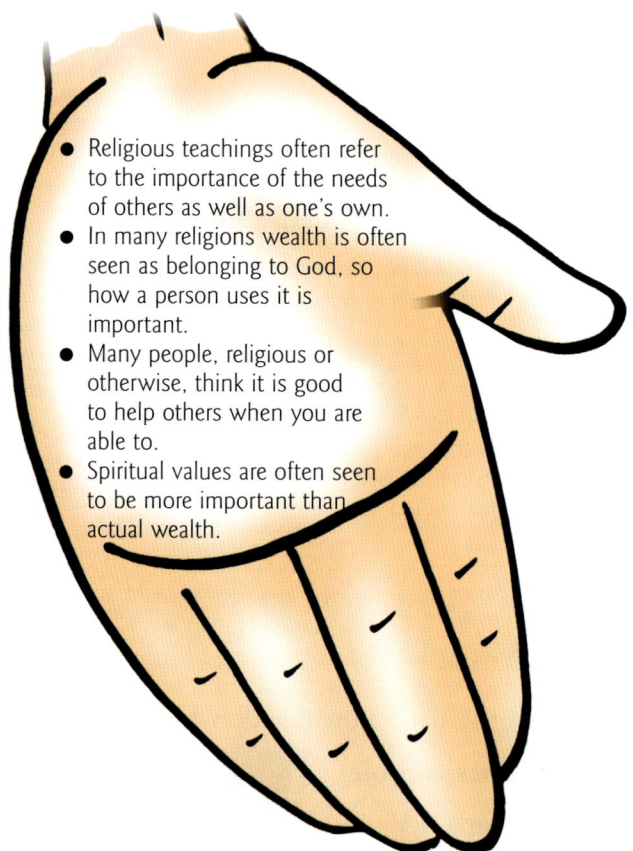

- Everyone has to look after themselves and their families, this is a duty even in many religious traditions.
- People should not rely on others to help them out all the time.
- How people choose to use their wealth is their own decision.
- When a person has worked hard and responsibly, they deserve to enjoy the benefits.

- Religious teachings often refer to the importance of the needs of others as well as one's own.
- In many religions wealth is often seen as belonging to God, so how a person uses it is important.
- Many people, religious or otherwise, think it is good to help others when you are able to.
- Spiritual values are often seen to be more important than actual wealth.

Exam Tip

Examination questions will often ask you about the work of individuals or groups. It is important that you always relate your answer to the impact of the person or group on the issue. As your answer will always be about a religious believer or organisation, it is important that you include how their faith has influenced or impacted on their actions.

> **Q** In this topic, question d) questions will often ask you about the IMPACT of the work of individuals or groups on issues of justice and equality. You could use the IMPACT formula below to help you organise your answer. An example has been done for Christian Aid.
>
> **I**dentify the correct name of the person or agency
>
> **M**ention the religious tradition to which they belong
>
> **P**récis the context in which the person or agency is working
>
> **A**cknowledge some of the main aspects of their work
>
> **C**onsider how their work demonstrates the teachings of the religion to which they belong
>
> **T**ell of specific examples of long- and short-term projects.

Example

d) Explain how a religious organisation has worked for Justice.

Identify: *What is Christian Aid?*

Christian Aid is a charity that supports people in over 60 countries.

Mention: *Which religion it belongs to*

Although Christian Aid promotes justice for people of all religions and of none, it is a Christian charity which is supported by more than 40 different denominations.

Précis: *What are the main aims?*

Christian Aid's main aim is to work towards a world where everyone can live a full life, free from poverty.

Acknowledge: *What are the main things they do?*

Christian Aid seeks justice and equal opportunities for all people. They do this through both urgent, practical support, such as emergency food relief, and by longer term work to improve the chances of the poorest people of the world, such as through teaching literacy and setting up health and vaccination clinics. They also campaign for fair trade and raise funds through events like Christian Aid Week.

Consider: *How the work of Christian Aid demonstrates the teachings of Christianity*

- Their work reflects the Christian belief that all people should treat others as they would like to be treated because God created everyone.
- They follow the example of Jesus through speaking out against injustice.
- Their work reflects the beliefs of the global Christian community. The Christian community will hold many fund-raising activities and offer prayers for the work of Christian Aid.

Tell: *Give a specific example of a project they are involved with*

In Senegal, Christian Aid works with local farmers to support their literacy and farming skills. They give access to money through loans at low rates so that people don't have to borrow money from corrupt loan dealers.

Activity

Now complete an IMPACT on how another religious person/organisation you have studied has worked for justice.

EXAMINATION PRACTICE

It is important that you understand the structure of the examination paper. This is explained in the Introduction on page 2.

Below are practice questions for each question type in the examination. After each of the questions there is a specimen answer which has been given a mark. Look at the levels of response grids on pages 67–8 and try to improve each answer to get full marks.

Question a) Explain what is meant by the term 'authority'. (*2 marks*)

Answer Having power.

(Level I = *I mark*)

Question b) Explain how having a religious faith might influence the way money is used. (*4 marks*)

Answer Most religious believers consider that you should treat others as you would like to be treated. In the Bible it teaches that material wealth isn't the most important thing in life.

(Level 3 = *3 marks*)

Question c) 'It's natural for people to have prejudices.' Give two reasons why a religious believer might agree or disagree with this statement. (*4 marks*)

Answer Everyone has prejudices because it is natural for people to have prejudices.

(Level 0 = *No marks*)

Question d) Explain how **one** person or religious organisation has worked for justice. (*6 marks*)

Answer Christian Aid has worked for justice by going abroad to help other people. They don't just give money away, they provide long-term projects that give people skills such as reading and trades. They campaign for many things.

(Level 2 = *2 marks*)

Question e) 'Giving to charity is throwing your money away.' Do you agree? Give reasons or evidence for your answer, showing that you have thought about more than one point of view. You must include references to religious beliefs in your answer. (*8 marks*)

Answer I don't agree because charity can help people less fortunate than yourself. It can be used to buy food or hospital equipment. Some people would say it is throwing money away because you don't know what happens to it.

(Level 2 = *3 marks*)

Topic 3 Looking for meaning

The Big Picture

Below is a summary of the key concepts, religious teachings and human experiences you need to know for the examination.

You need to know these!
The a) questions in the examination will ask you about these key concepts, *and* you should also use them in other questions as well.

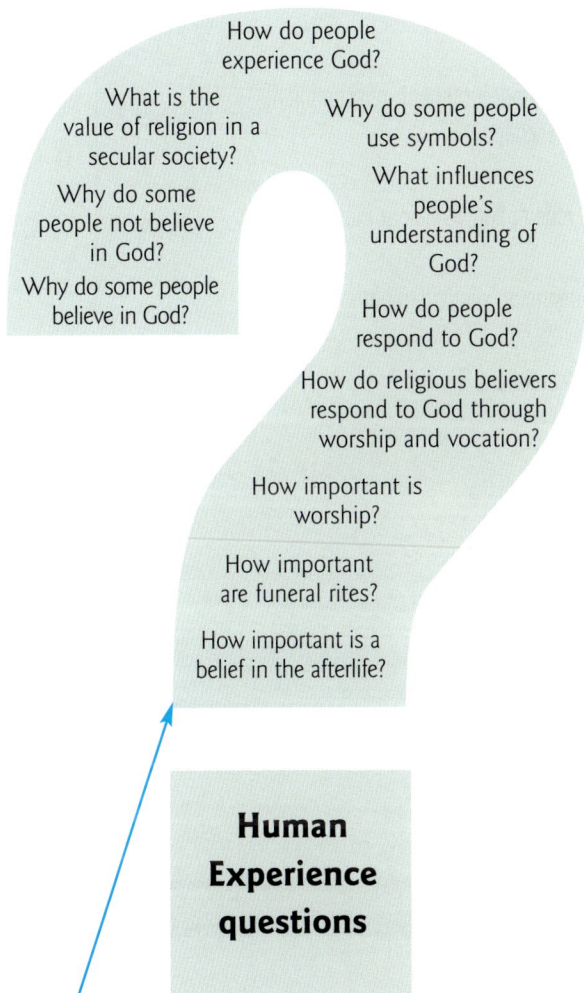

How do people experience God?

What is the value of religion in a secular society?

Why do some people use symbols?

Why do some people not believe in God?

What influences people's understanding of God?

Why do some people believe in God?

How do people respond to God?

How do religious believers respond to God through worship and vocation?

How important is worship?

How important are funeral rites?

How important is a belief in the afterlife?

Human Experience questions

Questions like these will be asked in c) and e) questions in the examination.

Key concepts to think about ▼

AFTERLIFE — AFTERLIFE

AWE

COMMUNITY

GOD — GOD

REVELATION

SYMBOLISM

Religious teachings to explore

- The nature of God
  - The nature of God or Ultimate Being
- The existence of God
  - Symbolism and imagery
  - Ideas about God
- Responses to God
  - Vocation
  - Acts of worship
- Religious teachings on death and the afterlife
- Religious funeral and mourning rites

The religious teachings here should be used in b), c), d), and e) questions. You need to know religious teachings for two traditions.

33

Religious and specialist terms

On the screen below are some religious and specialist terms you could use throughout the topic. You should be able to use terms from two different religious traditions or two denominations of Christianity. Definitions can be found in the Glossary on pages 69–70.

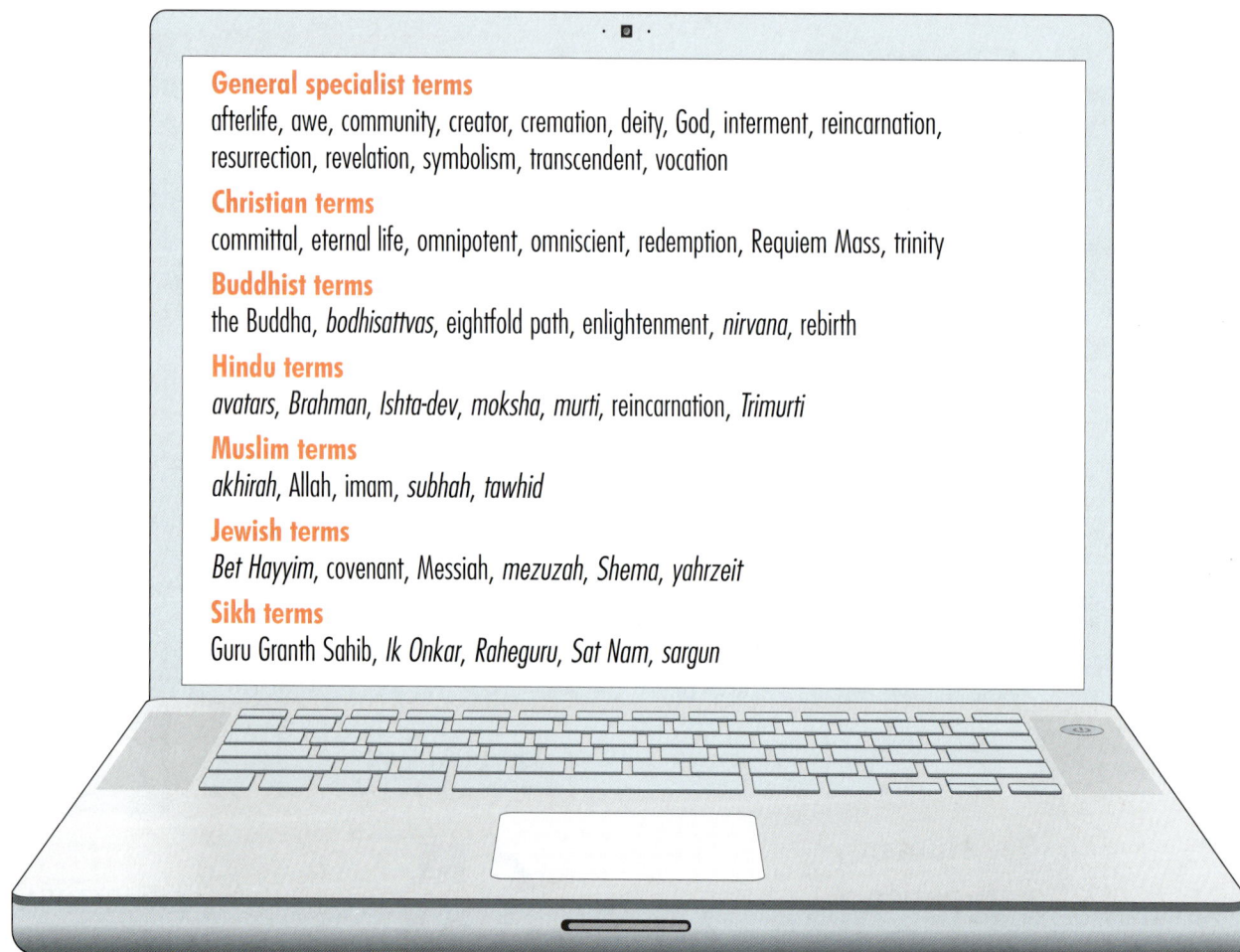

General specialist terms
afterlife, awe, community, creator, cremation, deity, God, interment, reincarnation, resurrection, revelation, symbolism, transcendent, vocation

Christian terms
committal, eternal life, omnipotent, omniscient, redemption, Requiem Mass, trinity

Buddhist terms
the Buddha, *bodhisattvas*, eightfold path, enlightenment, *nirvana*, rebirth

Hindu terms
avatars, *Brahman*, *Ishta-dev*, *moksha*, *murti*, reincarnation, *Trimurti*

Muslim terms
akhirah, Allah, imam, *subhah*, *tawhid*

Jewish terms
Bet Hayyim, covenant, Messiah, *mezuzah*, *Shema*, *yahrzeit*

Sikh terms
Guru Granth Sahib, *Ik Onkar*, *Raheguru*, *Sat Nam*, *sargun*

Exam Tip

It is important to use general specialist terms and terms from the religions you have studied in your answers to examination questions.

Exam Tip

If you can use stories or teachings from sacred texts to support your answer it will help you get high marks. You don't need to remember the exact words. You can make general references or put them in your own words.

Key concepts

There are six key concepts in this topic. The definition of each is shown in the keys below. The first examination question for each topic (question a)) will ask you to explain one of the key concepts for two marks. You should also refer to the key concepts in answers to other examination questions on the topic.

God

GOD

- Ultimate Being (creator and sustainer of the world).
- Deity (a visible form of the power behind the world).

Symbolism

Something that points to or explains something else. Religions have many symbolic actions and ideas.

Revelation

Something shown or explained that was previously hidden. Many religions have revealed truths, and these are important in the faith.

Awe

Completely overwhelmed by a sense of God's presence. In many religious traditions experiencing God or his presence is sought through various ways.

Community

A group of people with something in common, e.g. sharing the same faith, sharing in prayer and worship.

Afterlife

AFTERLIFE

The belief that there is some kind of life after the death of the body. Many religions have beliefs in a heaven or a place where souls or spirits go when the body dies.

Issues to consider

There are three main areas you will need to know about for this topic:
- issues about God's existence and nature
- issues about experiencing and responding to God
- issues about death and the afterlife – including funeral and mourning rites.

Issues about God's existence and nature

Religious teachings on God's existence and nature

In the examination, you may be asked questions on religious teachings and attitudes concerning God's nature and existence. These are normally b) and d) questions. You would need to answer from two different religious traditions. Many religions agree on the teachings shown in the 'general' box below.

Key religious teachings: the existence of God

GENERAL
Most traditions believe that there is some form of divine reality or ultimate being, who exists in a different way to humans and the universe.

CHRISTIANITY ✝
- God exists and always has done.
- The existence of the universe, the world and its inhabitants are proof of that.
- Religious experience and revelation also point to the reality of God.
- Jesus is the best way to know about God.

BUDDHISM ✵
- Buddhism has no concept of God or the existence of a divine being or ultimate reality.
- The essence of life is found in enlightenment, and the discovery of truth.

HINDUISM ॐ
- There is one God, an underlying spirit, called *Brahman*. He is in everything and everything is in him.
- There are hundreds of deities who are all manifestations (*avatars*) of *Brahman*.
- Three most well known deities are Brahma, Shiva and Vishnu.

ISLAM ☪
- Allah is the one true God, and from him all life comes.
- Allah has spoken to humanity through Prophet Muhammad.
- It is Allah that unites everything.

JUDAISM ✡
- God is creator of all, and is omnipotent (all-powerful), omniscient (all-knowing) and omnipresent (all-present).
- He is the one true God.

SIKHISM ☬
- God is one, who is the truth, and the creator of all that there is.
- God has no form, and cannot be depicted; but he is known by many names.

Key religious teachings: the nature of God and ideas about God

GENERAL

Most traditions believe that the true God is not only a creator, but has done or will do things to 'save' the world and the people in it.

CHRISTIANITY ✝

- God is one, but is known and experienced through three distinct persons: Father, Son and Holy Spirit. This is known as the Trinity.
- He is a God of love (like a father who cares) as well as judgement (who will reward and punish).
- He loves the world and all people in it, and sent his son Jesus to teach people about him, and to save people from their sins.
- Creator and sustainer of the world.
- Full of mercy and offers forgiveness to all willing to receiver it.
- Best known through Jesus.

BUDDHISM

- Buddhism does not have a belief in nor concept of a God or ultimate reality, therefore there are no teachings about his nature.

HINDUISM ॐ

- God is one, and is known as *Brahman*.
- He is in all things and all things are in him.
- There are many manifestations of *Brahman*.
- He is creator, destroyer as well as preserver of all.
- Everything is in him.

ISLAM ☪

- God is one, Allah.
- He created all things.
- Allah has many attributes, and some 99 names describe these.
- God is most merciful and will reward the faithful.
- He has spoken through the Prophet Muhammad.
- He will judge people according to their deeds.

JUDAISM

- God is a loving creator, and is one, the only true God.
- He sustains the earth and everything in it.
- He has chosen a covenant people (the Jews) and will send a Messiah to judge the world and resurrect the dead.

SIKHISM

- God is one, and timeless.
- He has no form or features, but is the Truth.
- His light pervades all things and leads to justice.
- Creator of all.
- Worshipped through service to others and in obeying his will.

Evaluation questions on God's existence and nature

There are four issues you should be able to evaluate. These are shown in the diagrams below and on page 39 and are often asked in c) and e) types of questions. Around the four issues in these diagrams are some views (both religious and non-religious) you could include in your answers.

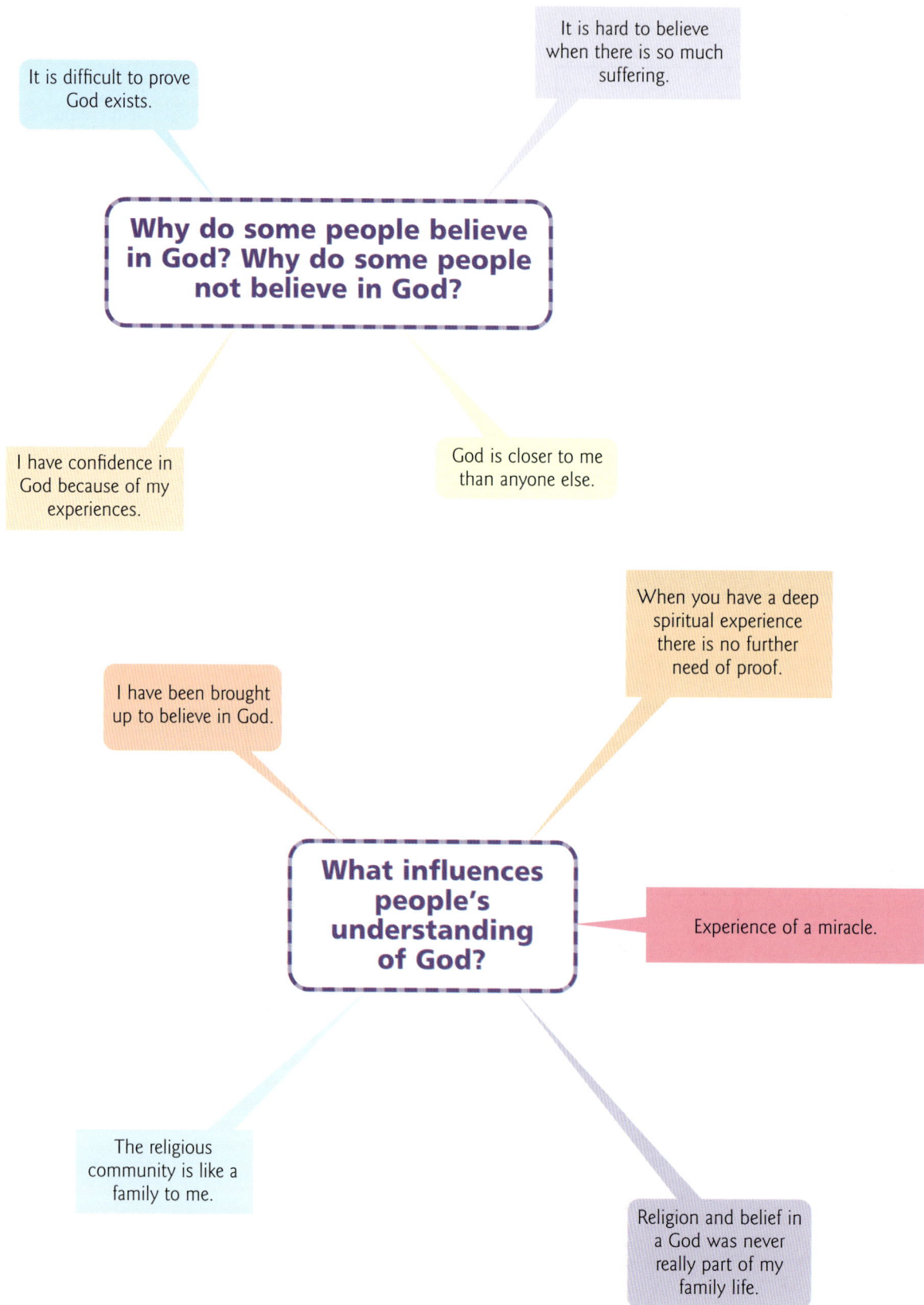

It is difficult to prove God exists.

It is hard to believe when there is so much suffering.

Why do some people believe in God? Why do some people not believe in God?

I have confidence in God because of my experiences.

God is closer to me than anyone else.

When you have a deep spiritual experience there is no further need of proof.

I have been brought up to believe in God.

What influences people's understanding of God?

Experience of a miracle.

The religious community is like a family to me.

Religion and belief in a God was never really part of my family life.

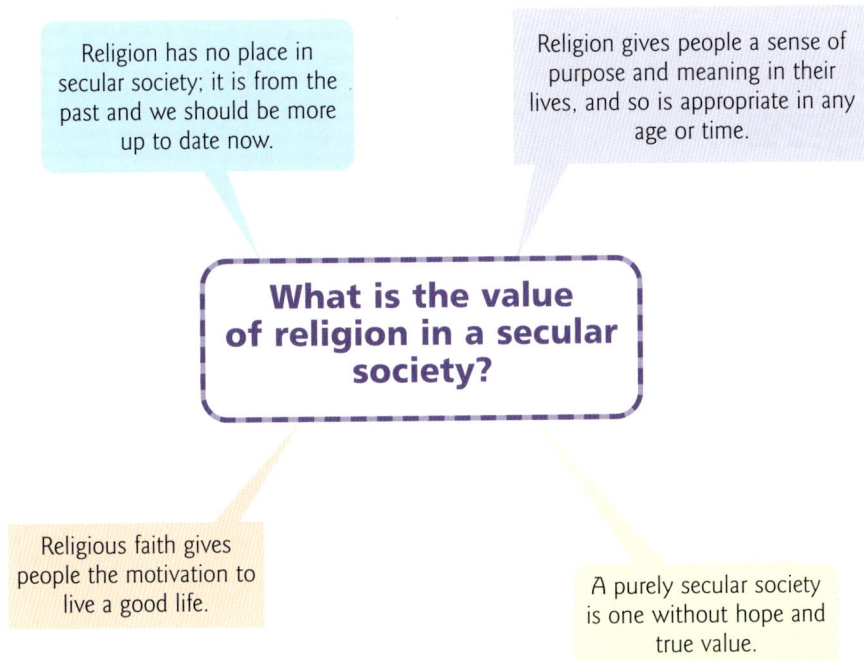

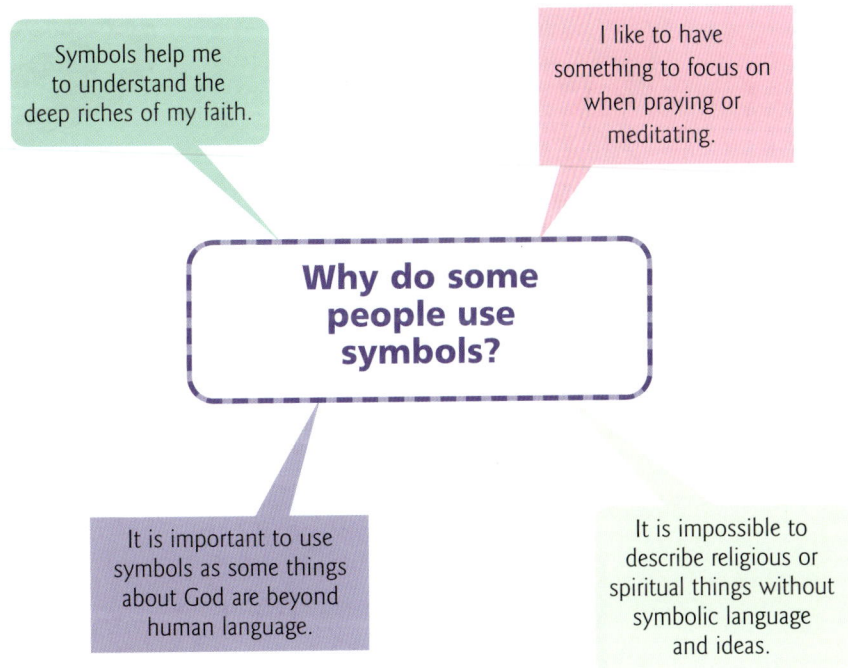

Religion has no place in secular society; it is from the past and we should be more up to date now.

Religion gives people a sense of purpose and meaning in their lives, and so is appropriate in any age or time.

What is the value of religion in a secular society?

Religious faith gives people the motivation to live a good life.

A purely secular society is one without hope and true value.

Symbols help me to understand the deep riches of my faith.

I like to have something to focus on when praying or meditating.

Why do some people use symbols?

It is important to use symbols as some things about God are beyond human language.

It is impossible to describe religious or spiritual things without symbolic language and ideas.

Exam Tip

Many religions include symbols that help believers understand and explain their faith. You need to be able to make reference to and explain these in your answers. On page 40 are common symbols from different religious traditions. Make sure you know what they mean in the religious traditions you are studying or are going to write about in the examination.

Religious symbols

Christian – crucifix. The crucifix reminds Christians of the death of Jesus on the cross, which they believe was for all people, and was the greatest act of love. His resurrection was the overcoming of sin and death, so the bringing of new life and hope to the world.

Buddhist – Eightfold path. The eight-spoke wheel represents the Noble Eightfold Path which Buddhists follow, and which helps them live life morally, with trained minds and an awareness of truth. This leads to the ultimate state – enlightenment.

Hindu – Ganesha. Ganesha, the elephant-headed deity, who is Lord of all Beings. His elephant head is a sign of strength, and he is the one to whom many Hindus pray for the removal of obstacles from their lives.

Muslim – *subhah* prayer beads. The *subhah* is a string of beads used to count recitations in worship. It has 99 beads on it, and each one represents one of the qualities of Allah. Many Muslims use it daily in their prayers as it helps them in their devotions and worship.

Jewish – *mezuzah*. The *mezuzah* case is found on the front door of many Jewish homes. It contains a copy of the words of the first two verses of the *Shema*, and reminds Jews of the oneness of God, and of his presence as they go about their daily lives.

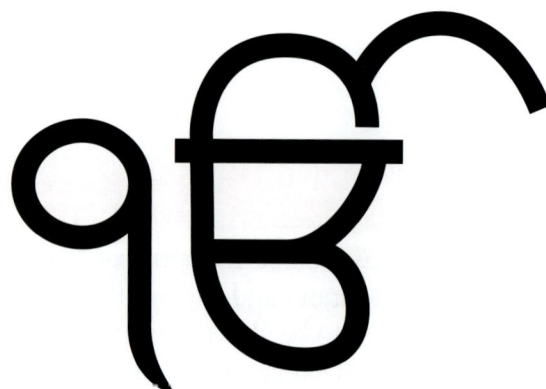

Sikh – *Ik Onkar*. This symbol comes from the opening letters of the *Mool Mantra* in the Sikh scriptures, and is a reminder to Sikhs of their central belief in the oneness of God. There are many names for God in Sikhism, but God is one, and he is everywhere and in everything.

40

Q 'Religion has no value in the modern world.' Do you agree? Give reasons or evidence for your answer showing that you have thought about more than one point of view. You must include references to religious beliefs in your answer.

Exam Tip

To gain full marks in evaluation e) questions you should include a range of moral and religious teachings in your arguments and include religious and general specialist language. Look at the points in each of the hands in answer to the question above and use them to help you to answer the question. Work out what specific religious terms from two different religious traditions you could add.

On the one hand ...

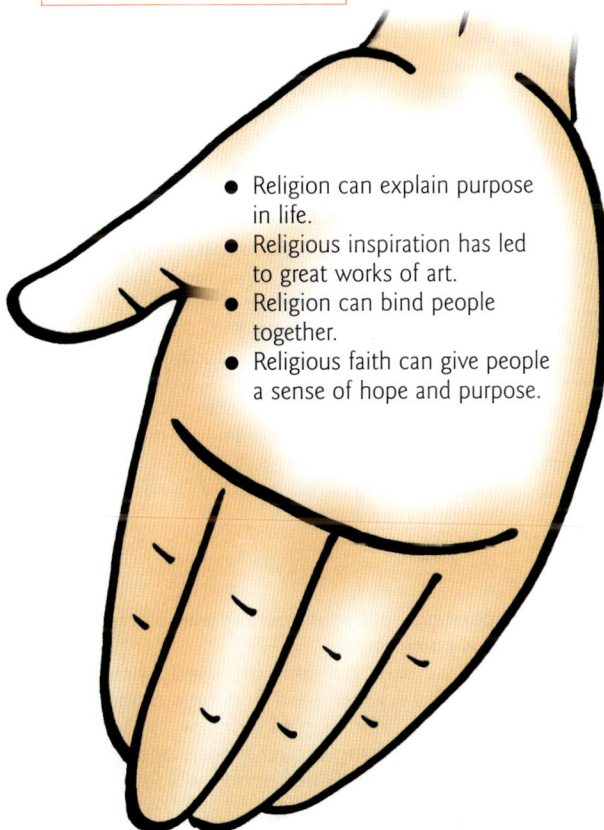

On the other hand ...

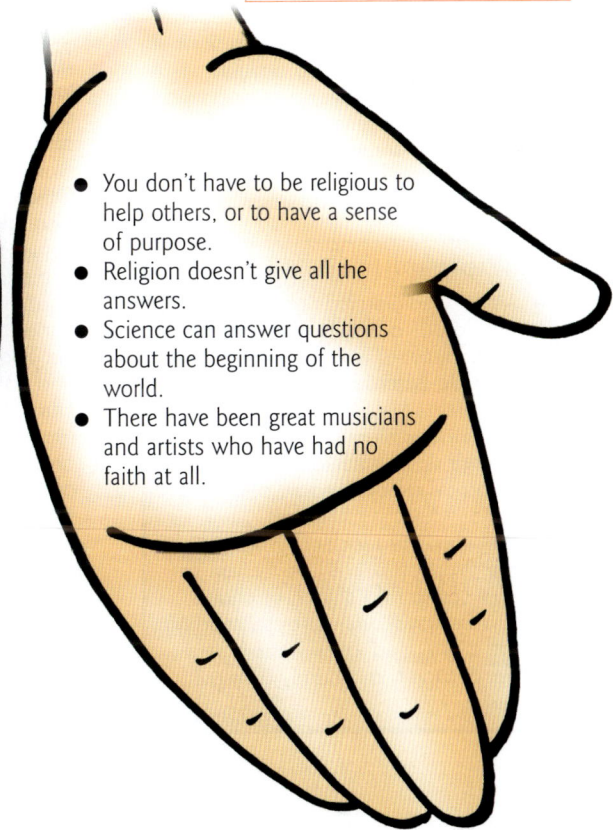

- Religion can explain purpose in life.
- Religious inspiration has led to great works of art.
- Religion can bind people together.
- Religious faith can give people a sense of hope and purpose.

- You don't have to be religious to help others, or to have a sense of purpose.
- Religion doesn't give all the answers.
- Science can answer questions about the beginning of the world.
- There have been great musicians and artists who have had no faith at all.

Issues about experiencing and responding to God

Religious teachings on acts of worship and vocation

In the examination, you may be asked questions on religious teachings and attitudes concerning acts of worship and vocation. These are normally b) and d) questions. You need to answer from two different religious traditions. Many religions agree on the teaching shown in the 'general' box below.

Key religious teachings: acts of worship

GENERAL
Most religions will refer to:
- Prayer: times for prayer, ways of praying, communal and private prayer.
- Preaching and teaching: helping believers to grow and develop in their faith, and as a witness to those outside of the community of faith.
- Worship: daily or regular, private or communal, involving different media.
- Pilgrimages: these are seen as acts of worship, and have special significance. They can be individual or communal.
- Service and commitment.
- Retreat or study: ways that religious believers can get away from normal responsibilities and so devote themselves to prayer.
- Vocation: the sense of 'calling' by God to do something, as a career or voluntary activity.

CHRISTIANITY ✝
- Most denominations observe Sunday as a holy day, and a time for communal worship. (Some observe Saturday, e.g. Seventh-day Adventists.)
- Some denominations will have Eucharist, communion or breaking of bread every Sunday; others on set Sundays in the month.
- Preaching or teaching (Ministry of the Word) is usually part of an act of worship in a church or chapel.
- Private devotions – prayer, reading the Bible, meditation – are encouraged, on a daily or regular basis.

HINDUISM ॐ
- *Puja* is a daily act of worship that most Hindus will observe in their own homes.
- Temples allow worship to be undertaken alone or communally.
- Offerings of fruit, flowers, and gifts are common in worship, as is the *arti* ceremony.

JUDAISM ✡
- *Shabbat* (the Sabbath day) is the Jewish day of worship (Friday sunset to Saturday sunset).
- The *Shabbat* ceremony takes place in the home and many Jews will attend the synagogue for worship on the Saturday.
- Other acts of worship also take place in the home, such as *Havdalah* (the ending of the Sabbath), ceremonies during the year (such as the *Seder* meal at *Pesach*, and lighting lights at *Hanukkah*) and the regular daily times of prayer (morning, afternoon and evening).

ISLAM ☪
- Muslims pray five times a day (*salah*) at set times, and face towards Makkah when performing the *rak'ahs* (prayer positions).
- Prayers can take place anywhere, and prayer mats are commonly used when not in the mosque.
- Washing (*wudu*) before prayer is always performed.
- *Jumma* prayers take place in the mosque, often on Fridays.

SIKHISM ☬
- Worship in Sikhism is also personal, and reciting, reading from the Guru Granth Sahib, reciting *Japji* and other prayers, and use of mala beads are common activities.
- Sikh communities usually gather regularly in the *gurdwara*, listen to readings and explanations, sing hymns, and share in *karah parshad* (sacred food) and a communal meal in the *langar*.

BUDDHISM ☸
- Worship is mainly personal, although joining with others in temples and shrines is common.
- There is no set day for worship, but there are special times and festivals, such as *Wesak* which most Buddhists observe.
- Offering of fruit and flowers, chanting of mantras, meditating, burning incense, using prayer wheels and prayer flags are also common activities during worship.

Evaluation questions on experiencing and responding to God

There are four issues you should be able to evaluate. These are shown in the diagrams below and on page 44 and are often asked in c) and e) types of questions. Around the four issues in the diagrams are some views (both religious and non-religious) you could include in your answers.

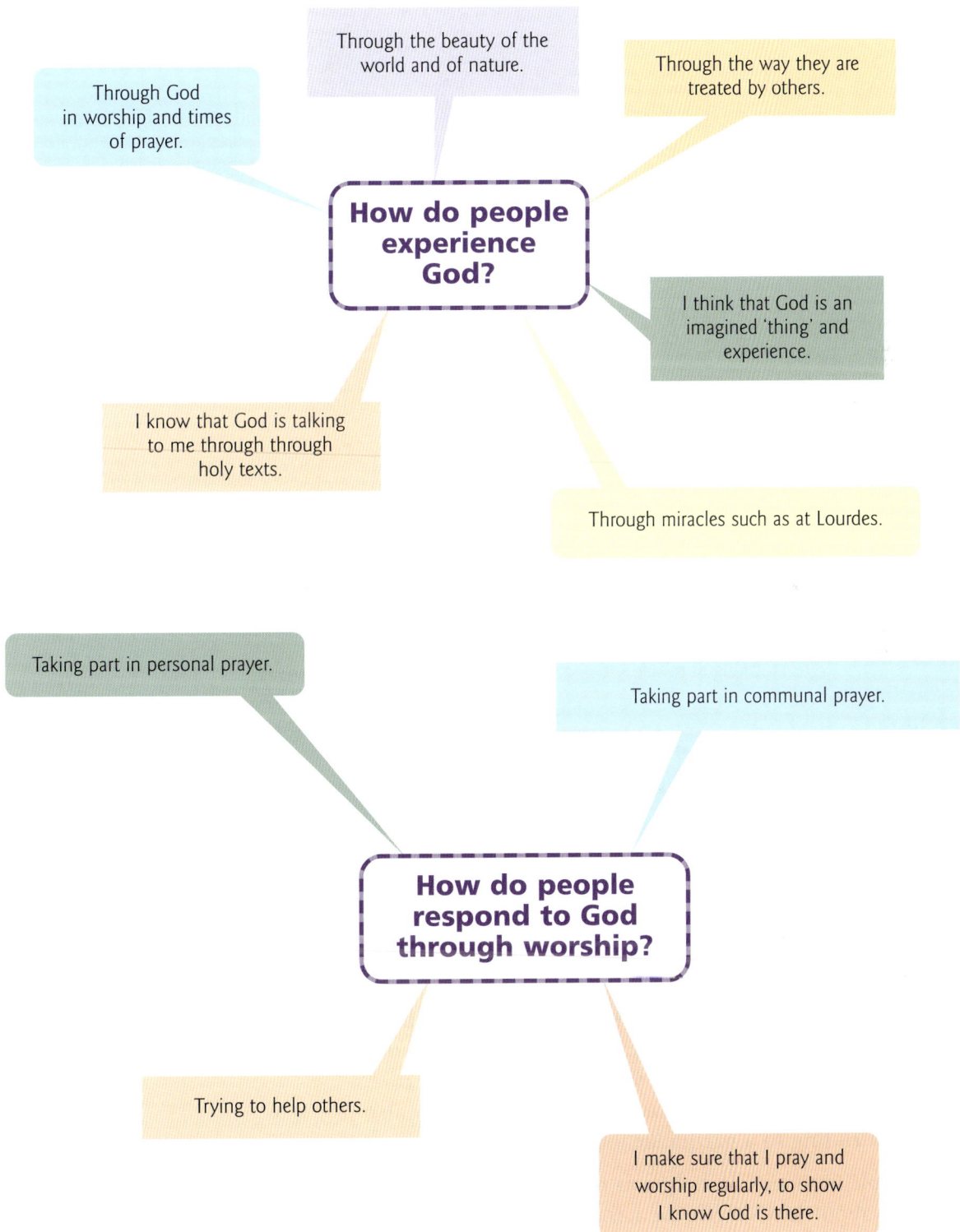

Through the beauty of the world and of nature.

Through God in worship and times of prayer.

Through the way they are treated by others.

How do people experience God?

I think that God is an imagined 'thing' and experience.

I know that God is talking to me through through holy texts.

Through miracles such as at Lourdes.

Taking part in personal prayer.

Taking part in communal prayer.

How do people respond to God through worship?

Trying to help others.

I make sure that I pray and worship regularly, to show I know God is there.

I owe everything to Christ; so I try to live my life for him, and in the way he asks – this is my calling as a Christian.

God calls all believers to worship only him, and to look after his world. This is their duty.

How do religious believers respond to God through vocation?

I chose my job as a teacher so that I could help others.

God is the centre of my life – after all, he gave me all things to enjoy; and I serve others too – it is my duty.

I have renounced everything of the world and its pleasures, and live my life through service.

For me teaching and preaching to others is my response to all that God has done for me.

To go on a pilgrimage is a wonderful experience, but it is also a response to what God has done for me.

How important is worship?

I find worship is hard, but it is something that you learn how to do over time.

You can worship on you own; you don't have to do it with others.

Worship and prayer are the centre of my life.

For some religions worship is a duty.

Activity

Vocation is not a word much used in everyday language, but you need to be able to understand it, and both use the term and explain what religious believers mean by it.

For religious people vocation is the way they do things in their everyday life, their sense of calling to live their lives in a certain way – and this is their response to God or the 'faith' they have. Sometimes that may also mean a calling to a particular job or career.

A simple acrostic can help you remember the key things about it. Compile an acrostic for VOCATION – to help you remember what it is about.

Q 'Worship is pointless.' Do you agree? Give reasons or evidence for your answer, showing that you have thought about more than one point of view. You must refer to religious beliefs in your answer.

Exam Tip

To gain full marks in evaluation e) questions you should include a range of moral and religious teachings in your arguments and include religious and general specialist language. Look at the points in each of the hands in answer to the question above and use them to help you to answer the question. Work out what specific religious terms from two different religious traditions you could add.

On the one hand …

On the other hand …

- Prayer and worship often inspire people to greater things; they become aware of more than just themselves. Believers feel a responsibility to their God or faith.
- Worship brings people in the community together, and helps support individuals in their lives and their faith.
- Worship often enables believers to do things for the benefit of others – such as serving the community or those in need.

- Worship is merely a ritual that people go through and has no actual benefit. Believers meet together and go through various actions – that is all.
- Worshipping together in special places divides the community and separates people out according to religion.
- Even when serving others, religious believers are really doing it because they hope to gain some merit through it.

Issues about death and the afterlife

Religious teachings on death, the afterlife and funeral rites

In the examination, you may be asked questions on religious teachings and attitudes concerning death, the afterlife and funeral rites. These are normally b) and d) questions. You need to answer from two different religious traditions. The key religious teachings are outlined below. Many religions agree on the teachings shown in the 'general' box below.

Key religious teachings: death and the afterlife

GENERAL
- Most religious traditions believe there is some form of life after death, which needs to be prepared for during life.
- All religious traditions have some form of rituals or ceremonies surrounding death.

CHRISTIANITY ✝
- There is eternal life after death, which is received through faith.
- Entry to heaven depends on a person's response to Jesus, and to those in need on earth.
- Resurrection is expected, because of the resurrection of Jesus.
- There is a hell – the opposite of heaven – a place of separation from God.

Roman Catholic churches
- The souls of very good believers will go directly to heaven.
- Most other believers will go to purgatory, a place of cleansing that is between earth and heaven.
- Prayers can be said for those in purgatory to shorten their stay there, and intercessions can be made through indulgences and penance.

HINDUISM ॐ
- Reincarnation, or the rebirth of the *atman* into another body, takes place after death.
- *Moksha* (salvation) is eventually reached, where the *atman* is reunited with Brahman.

JUDAISM ♆
- Resurrection of soul and body is part of most Jewish ideas about life after death.
- Everyone will be judged, and those who led good lives will be close to God; others will be purified in hell.

BUDDHISM ☸
- Rebirth is the key to breaking away from the endless cycle of birth, growth, decay and death.
- *Nirvana* is a state of mind where greed, ignorance and hatred cease.

ISLAM ☪
- *Akhirah* (life after death) is determined by one's deeds on earth.
- The soul is released straight after death.
- Hell and paradise are described in the Qur'an; paradise is for believers who live righteously.

SIKHISM ☬
- The soul is immortal, and a good person will gain *mukti*, which is release from the cycle of rebirths.
- Death is part of life for everyone, but returning to God is expected through leading a good life.

Many religions agree on the teachings shown in the 'general' box below.

Key religious teachings: funeral rites

GENERAL

Most traditions have ideas about:
- showing respect to the body of the dead person.
- burying or cremating the body.
- celebrating the life of the person who has died.
- rehearsing the beliefs in the life after death and the future progress of the 'soul'.

CHRISTIANITY ✝

- Interment (burial) is a choice for many Christians, with a cross or memorial stone placed over the grave.
- Many choose cremation, and the ashes are scattered, or sometimes buried in a special box.
- A funeral service may include a Eucharist or a Mass.
- Most funerals will include Bible readings, hymns, and reference to the resurrection and new life.

Roman Catholic churches
- Funerals often include a Requiem Mass.
- Priests wear white robes; white is the colour for life after death and the resurrection.
- Coffins are sprinkled with holy water at the door of the church.

HINDUISM ॐ

- Cremation is always preferred, as it helps to release the *atman* (soul). Only *Sadhus* (holy men) and children may be buried.
- Scriptures are read, and symbolic offerings of water and rice cakes to ancestors take place.
- Ashes are scattered in running water (many go to the River Ganges in India for this).

ISLAM ☪

- The imam leads prayers in the mosque and at the grave.
- Bodies are usually buried within 24 hours of death.
- *Hajji* (men who have been on *hajj*) will be buried in their *ihram* (robe).

JUDAISM 🕎

- Sometimes a *tallit* (prayer shawl) with one of the fringes cut is placed over the body.
- Funerals usually take place within 24 hours of death.
- Prayers and psalms will be read, and each person may put a spadeful of earth in the grave, a symbol of returning to the earth.

SIKHISM ☬

- The body is washed with water and yoghurt before being dressed.
- In India, bodies are usually cremated, in the UK they are buried.
- *Ardas* (closing prayers) are said as the body is burned or buried.
- No monuments or memorials are used.

BUDDHISM ☸

- Monks are usually involved in the rituals after death.
- Bodies are usually cremated, and this shows the finality of death.
- Often relatives and friends will give alms (*dana*) as part of their own journey towards *nirvana* as well as helping that of their relative who has died.

Exam Tip

You will be expected to be able to explain the funeral rites and beliefs in the afterlife for the two traditions you have studied. A useful way of remembering the key beliefs is an acrostic. There are some examples on page 48 – use them to help you recall the main features of the two traditions you will be answering about.

Christianity

E ternal life received through faith.

T iming of death in God's hands.

E ntry to heaven depends on response to Jesus, and to people in need.

R esurrection is the main theme of funeral services.

N ew heaven and earth will be made after judgement day.

A fter life is a spiritual experience.

L ife choices very important; hell = separation from God by personal choice.

L iving a life of love towards others is the way to eternal life.

I nterment (burial) chosen by some; cremation by others.

F unerals may include a Eucharist or a Mass; hymns and Bible readings too.

E nding is with words of committal: earth to earth, ashes to ashes.

Buddhism

R ecognising that all things are impermanent is important.

E scaping the endless cycle of life is the goal through the eightfold path.

B ad follows bad, good follows good; this law affects present and future.

I gnorance, greed and hatred need extinguishing to gain enlightenment.

R ebirth is not a person being reborn but karmic energy of the person which sets another life into being.

T he goal of Buddhists is *nirvana* – a state of contentment beyond the physical cravings of the body.

H elping the deceased through transferring merit to them is done through special ceremonies.

Hinduism

R etirement or renunciation are stages in life to help prepare for death.

E uthanasia and extending of life disapproved – natural ending is best.

I mmediate family carry out rituals after death – water, tulsi leaf, *antyyesti*.

N ext day funeral takes place – taken by priest or eldest son.

C remation preferred – it releases *atman*; only *sadhus* or children are buried.

A shes scattered on running water; Ganges if possible.

R ituals bring peace to departed soul; *shraddha* – offering water, rice cakes.

N ear relatives gather for reading of scriptures

A nnual commemorations held.

T ransmigration (reincarnation) is *atman* entering a new body.

E scaping cycle of rebirths (*moksha*) through pure life is hoped for.

Islam

A llah knows the time of a person's death.

K indness should be shown to the dying by helping them recite *Shahadah*.

H ajji will have their *ihram* draped over them.

I mam leads prayers in the mosque and graveside; funeral within 24 hours.

R elease of the soul happens straight after death.

A ngels record people's deeds during life; this is used at judgement day.

H ell and paradise are described; the righteous and faithful go to paradise.

Judaism

R esurrection of the soul is believed in by most Jews.

E uthanasia and autopsies are disapproved of.

S ynagogues play an important role in funerals; *Chevra Kaddisha* prepare.

U sually funerals within 24 hours of death.

R abbi conducts ceremony at cemetery (*Bet Hayyim*); prayers, psalms read.

R esurrection of dead believed in; 'House of Life' is meaning of *Bet Hayyim*.

E veryone throws spadeful of earth on the coffin – symbol of return to the earth.

C are of the living is important; close family support the bereaved members.

T ombstones are consecrated; stones not flowers put on grave.

I mmortality of the soul is believed in by most Jews.

O bservance of the anniversary of death is usual (*yahrzeit*).

N ames of the dead sometimes placed on plaques in synagogue.

Sikhism

N o cooking done in house on day someone has died.

E very person has part of God in them, so will return to him.

W ashing of the body in water and yoghurt before it is dressed.

D eath seen as within the will of God, and opportunity for rebirth.

A rdas or closing prayers said as body burnt.

W hen body has been burnt, ashes taken and sprinkled on running water.

N o monuments or stones allowed.

Evaluation questions on death and the afterlife

There are two issues you should be able to evaluate. These are shown in the diagrams below and are often asked in c) and e) types of questions. Around the two issues in the diagrams below are some views (both religious and non-religious) you could include in your answers.

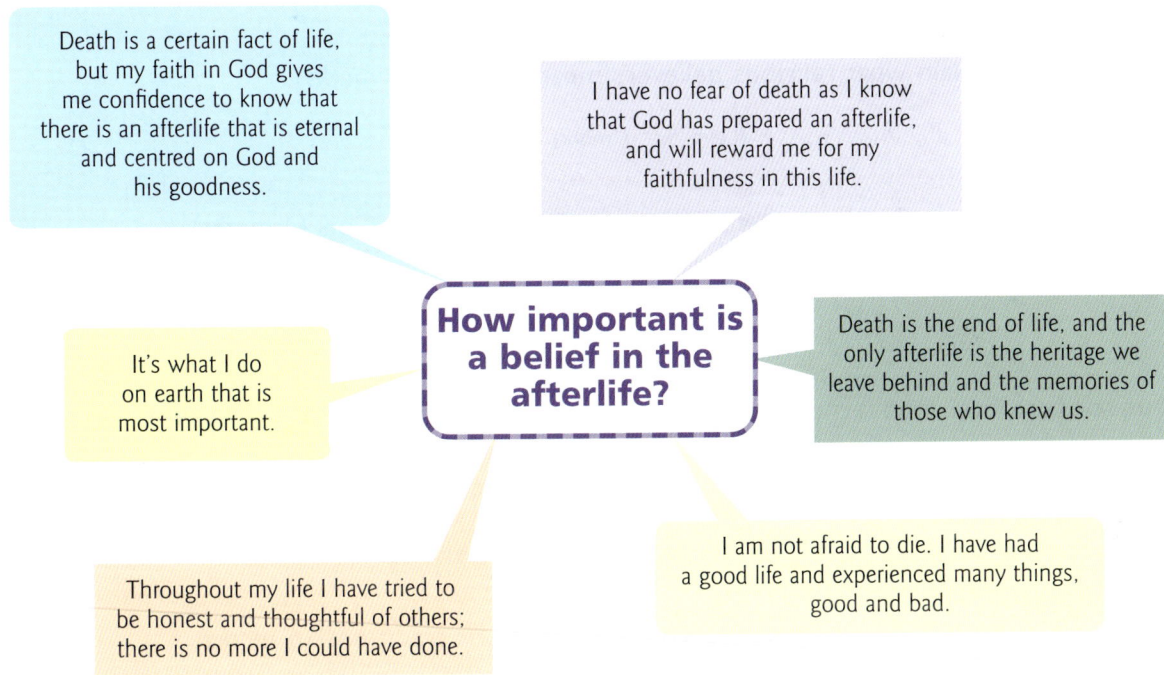

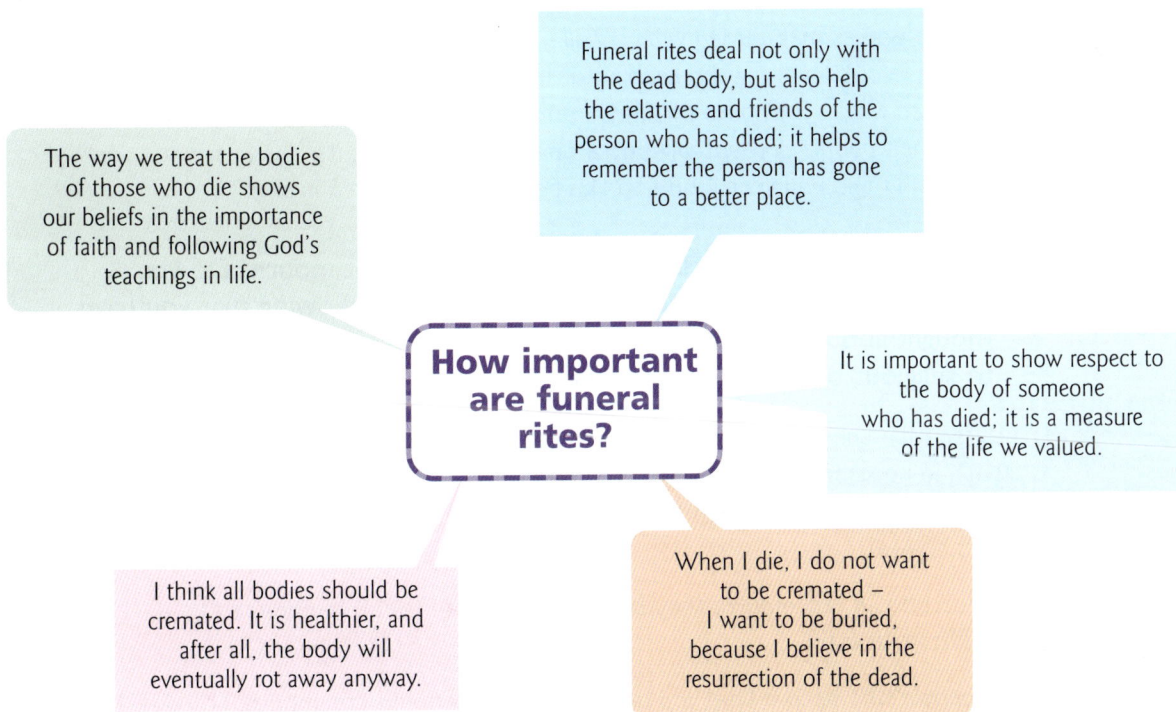

Death is a certain fact of life, but my faith in God gives me confidence to know that there is an afterlife that is eternal and centred on God and his goodness.

I have no fear of death as I know that God has prepared an afterlife, and will reward me for my faithfulness in this life.

It's what I do on earth that is most important.

How important is a belief in the afterlife?

Death is the end of life, and the only afterlife is the heritage we leave behind and the memories of those who knew us.

Throughout my life I have tried to be honest and thoughtful of others; there is no more I could have done.

I am not afraid to die. I have had a good life and experienced many things, good and bad.

Funeral rites deal not only with the dead body, but also help the relatives and friends of the person who has died; it helps to remember the person has gone to a better place.

The way we treat the bodies of those who die shows our beliefs in the importance of faith and following God's teachings in life.

How important are funeral rites?

It is important to show respect to the body of someone who has died; it is a measure of the life we valued.

I think all bodies should be cremated. It is healthier, and after all, the body will eventually rot away anyway.

When I die, I do not want to be cremated – I want to be buried, because I believe in the resurrection of the dead.

49

EXAMINATION PRACTICE

It is important that you understand the structure of the examination paper. This is explained in the Introduction on page 2. Below are practice questions for each question type in the examination. After each of the questions there is a specimen answer which has been given a mark. Look at the levels of response grids on pages 67–8 and try to improve each answer to get full marks.

Question a) Explain what religious believers mean by 'awe'. (*2 marks*)

> **Answer** Really afraid of God.   (*Level 1 = 1 mark*)

Question b) Explain how religious believers might experience God. (*4 marks*)

> **Answer** Religious believers might feel they have experienced God through worship they have taken part in, such as a Hindu in *puja*.   (*Level 2 = 2 marks*)

Question c) 'Everyone has to respond to God at some time or other.' Give **two** reasons why religious believers might agree or disagree. (*4 marks*)

> **Answer** Saying the world is a wonderful place is a response to God. Everyone searches for something when facing hard times in life.   (*Level 2 = 2 marks*)

Question d) Explain the funeral rites from **two** religious traditions. (*6 marks*)

> **Answer** Christians can choose burial or cremation. Most funeral services will include Bible readings, hymns and reminders about the resurrection and new life. Sometimes, there will be a cross or memorial stone, or after a cremation, the ashes may be scattered, buried in a special box, or kept in a jar or urn.
>
> Jews are sometimes buried with a *tallit* placed over the body, with one of the fringes cut to show the keeping of their duties. The funeral will usually take place within 24 hours of death, and prayers and psalms will be read. Sometimes people present will put a spadeful of earth into the grave, symbolising the body returning to the earth   (*Level 4 = 5 marks*)

Question e) 'People who believe life belongs to God should not mourn.' Do you agree? Give reasons or evidence for your answer, showing that you have thought about more than one point of view. You must include references to religious beliefs in your answer. (8 marks)

> **Answer** I agree with the statement. If you believe God is in charge of life, then death is no accident. Most Christians believe God loves them and has a plan for their lives. So when they die, earthly life finishes; they are in a new life in heaven.
>
> Hindus should not mourn; they believe the *atman* (soul) is released to a new life at death.
>
> So, people who believe that life belongs to God should not mourn.
> (*Level 2 = 4 marks*)

Topic 4 Our world

The Big Picture

Below is a summary of the key concepts, religious teachings and human experiences you need to know for the examination.

You need to know these!
The a) questions in the examination will ask you about these key concepts, *and* you should also use them in other questions as well.

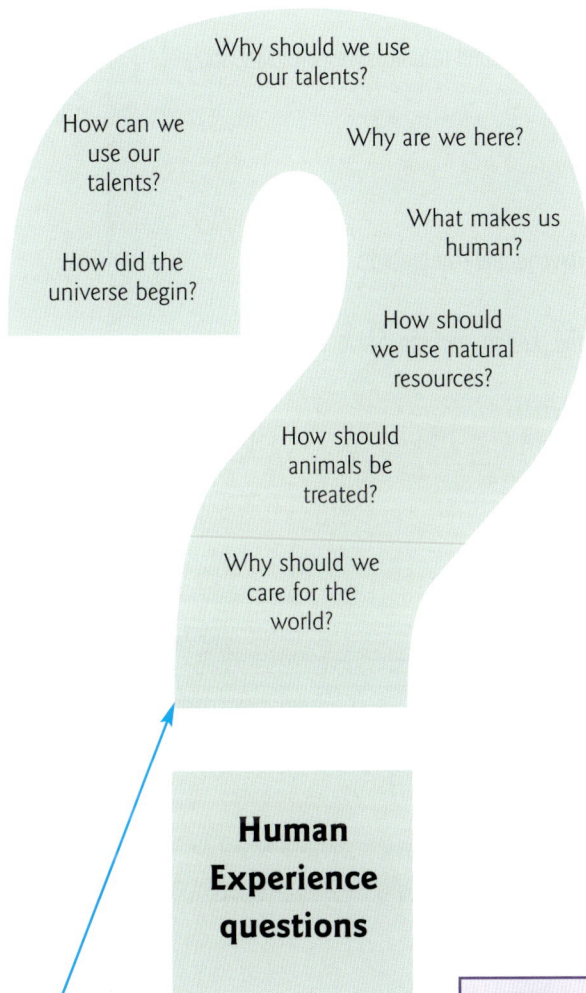

Why should we use our talents?

How can we use our talents?

Why are we here?

What makes us human?

How did the universe begin?

How should we use natural resources?

How should animals be treated?

Why should we care for the world?

Human Experience questions

Questions like these will be asked in c) and e) questions in the examination.

Key concepts to think about ▼

CREATION

DOMINION

ENVIRONMENT

HUMANITY

SOUL

STEWARDSHIP

Religious teachings to explore
- Creation
  - Creation stories and their meaning
- Using talents
- Place of humankind in the world
  - Purpose of humankind in the world
  - Stewardship issues in terms of the current exploitation of the planet
- Animal rights
- Care for the world and the environment
  - Example of a religious individual or community using talents for God, neighbour and care of the planet

The religious teachings here should be used in b), c), d), and e) questions. You need to know religious teachings for two traditions.

Religious and specialist terms

On the screen below are some religious and specialist terms you could use throughout the topic. You should be able to use terms from two different religious traditions or two denominations of Christianity. Definitions can be found in the Glossary on pages 69–70.

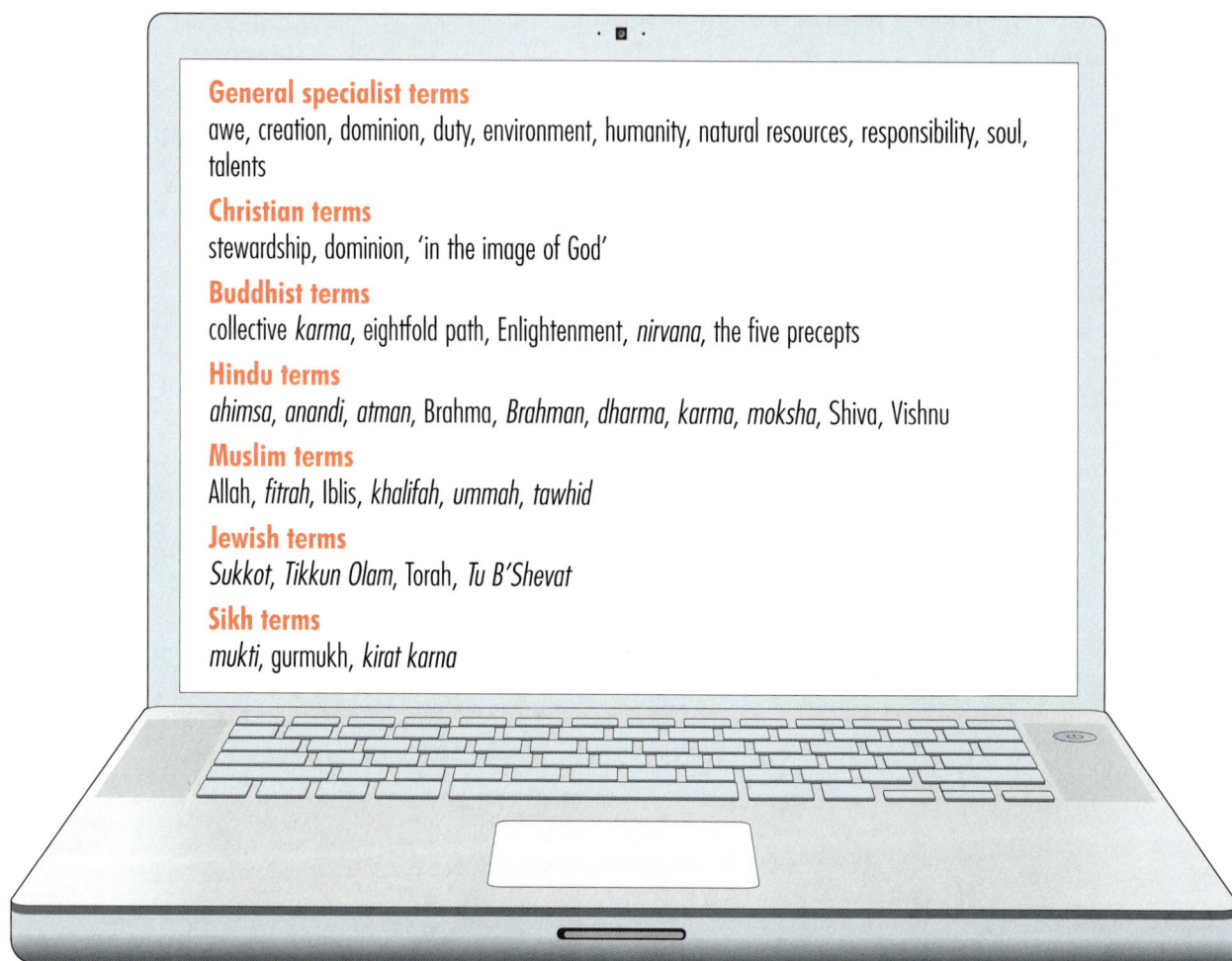

General specialist terms
awe, creation, dominion, duty, environment, humanity, natural resources, responsibility, soul, talents

Christian terms
stewardship, dominion, 'in the image of God'

Buddhist terms
collective *karma*, eightfold path, Enlightenment, *nirvana*, the five precepts

Hindu terms
ahimsa, anandi, atman, Brahma, *Brahman, dharma, karma, moksha*, Shiva, Vishnu

Muslim terms
Allah, *fitrah*, Iblis, *khalifah, ummah, tawhid*

Jewish terms
Sukkot, Tikkun Olam, Torah, *Tu B'Shevat*

Sikh terms
mukti, gurmukh, *kirat karna*

Exam Tip

It is important to use general specialist terms and terms from the religions you have studied in your answers to examination questions.

Exam Tip

If you can use stories or teachings from sacred texts to support your answer it will help you get high marks. You don't need to remember the exact words. You can make general references or put them in your own words.

Key concepts

There are six key concepts in this topic. The definition of each is shown in the keys below. The first examination question for each topic (question a)) will ask you to explain one of the key concepts for two marks. You should also refer to the key concepts in answers to other examination questions on the topic.

Creation
Making something deliberately, for a purpose. Most religions teach that the world was created by God for a purpose.

Dominion
Being in charge of the world for God. Some religions teach that God gave humans a responsibility to manage the world on his behalf.

Environment
The natural world all about us: plants, insects, animals and humans. Most religions believe that God created the world and everything in it.

Humanity
Caring for other human beings. Many religions teach that it is expected that human beings will care for each other, and show kindness to others.

Soul
The part of humans that lives on after the body has died. Some religions teach that there is a spiritual side of life that lives on beyond physical death.

Stewardship
To look after and care for the world. Most religions teach that humans have a God-given responsibility to look after the world.

Issues to consider

There are four main areas you will need to know about for this topic:
- issues about creation and the beginning of the universe
- issues about the place of humankind in the world
- issues about animal rights
- issues about care for the world and the environment.

Issues about creation and the beginning of the universe

Religious teachings on creation and the beginning of the universe

In the examination, you may be asked questions on religious teachings and attitudes concerning issues of creation and the beginning of the universe. These are normally b) and d) questions. You need to answer from two different religious traditions. The key religious teachings are outlined below and on page 55. It is important that you remember that there will be different views and practices between believers in the same tradition.

Christianity and Judaism

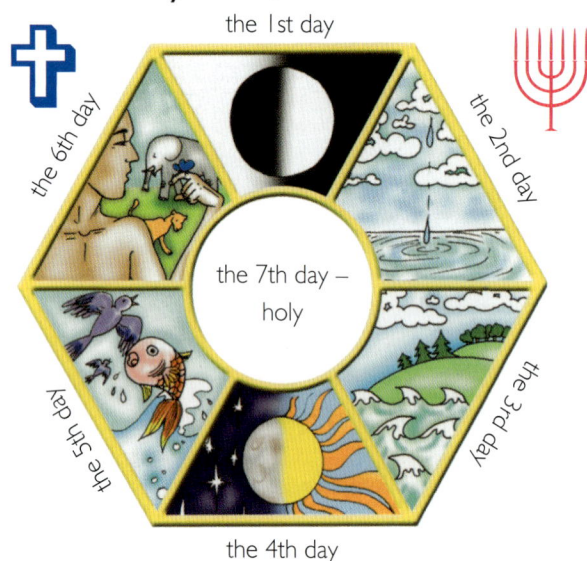

the 1st day
the 2nd day
the 3rd day
the 4th day
the 5th day
the 6th day
the 7th day – holy

The main points of the creation story are:
- God created the world, and it was fundamentally good
- there is a purpose to existence
- human beings have a special relationship to God and to the world.

Exam Tip

Be sure that your answers do not just describe the story, but explain what the meaning behind the story is – that is the real religious teaching about the beginnings of the universe behind the story itself.

Buddhism

In Buddhism there is no creation story, as:
- there is no belief in a creator being
- the universe has always existed
- life is a cycle of births and deaths, changing and developing
- endless discussion on how the universe began is pointless
- what matters is living life to reach enlightenment and *nirvana*.

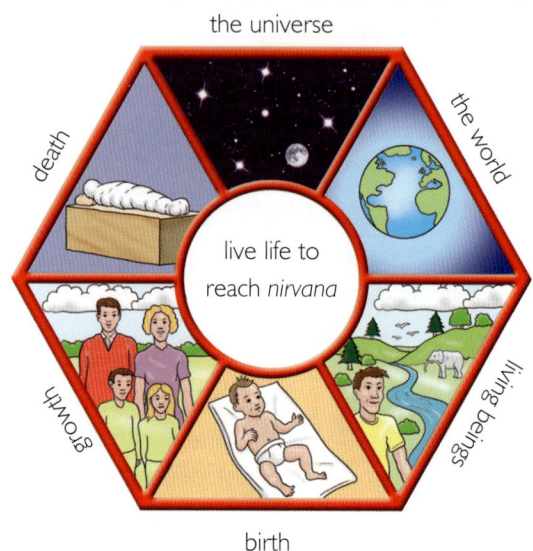

the universe
the world
living beings
birth
growth
death
live life to reach *nirvana*

Hinduism

Brahma – creator

Vishnu – preserver

Shiva – destroyer

humans

animals

plants

life is a cycle of existences

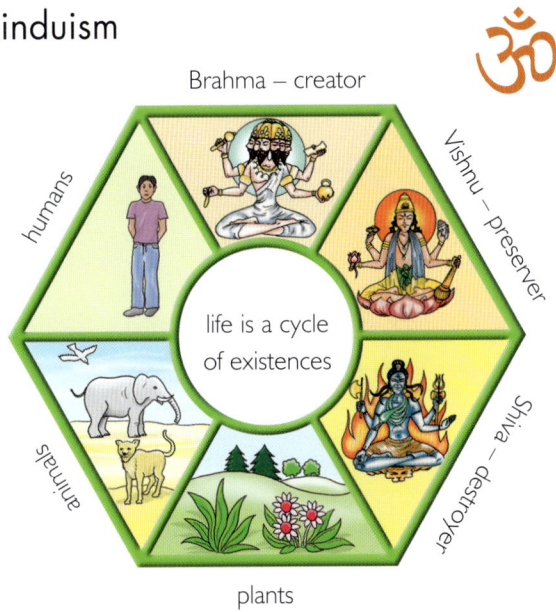

Creation in Hinduism is *anandi* – that which has no beginning. However, there is a cycle to existence:
* things come to life (birth) – and Brahma creates all life
* lives are led through growth and development – and Vishnu sustains all things
* things come to an end (death) – and Shiva brings things to their end at the appropriate time
* the object of life is to live so as to obtain *moksha* – release from the endless cycle of existence.

Islam

In Islam it is believed that Allah created all things, and the main points of the creation story in Islam are as follows:
* Allah made the world and everything in it
* humans were given the role of *khalifahs* or stewards and have a binding responsibility to look after the world and treat it with respect
* on the day of judgment all Muslims will be called into account for how they have looked after Allah's creation.

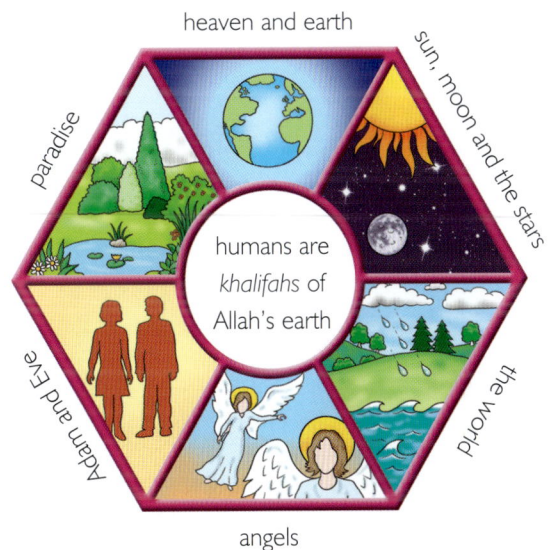

heaven and earth

sun, moon and the stars

paradise

the world

Adam and Eve

angels

humans are *khalifahs* of Allah's earth

Sikhism

deep darkness

the universe

human beings

the earth

birds and animals

the environment

God is present in all of his creation

Sikhs believe the world was brought into being deliberately by God. The story shows that:
* God is present in all things that he created
* the creation is his gift of love
* the world and life are to be enjoyed
* God meant the world and humans to grow, develop and evolve.

Evaluation questions on creation and the beginning of the universe

There is one issue you should be able to evaluate. This is shown in the diagram below and is often asked about in c) and e) types of questions. Around the issue in the diagram below are some views (both religious and non-religious) you could include in your answer.

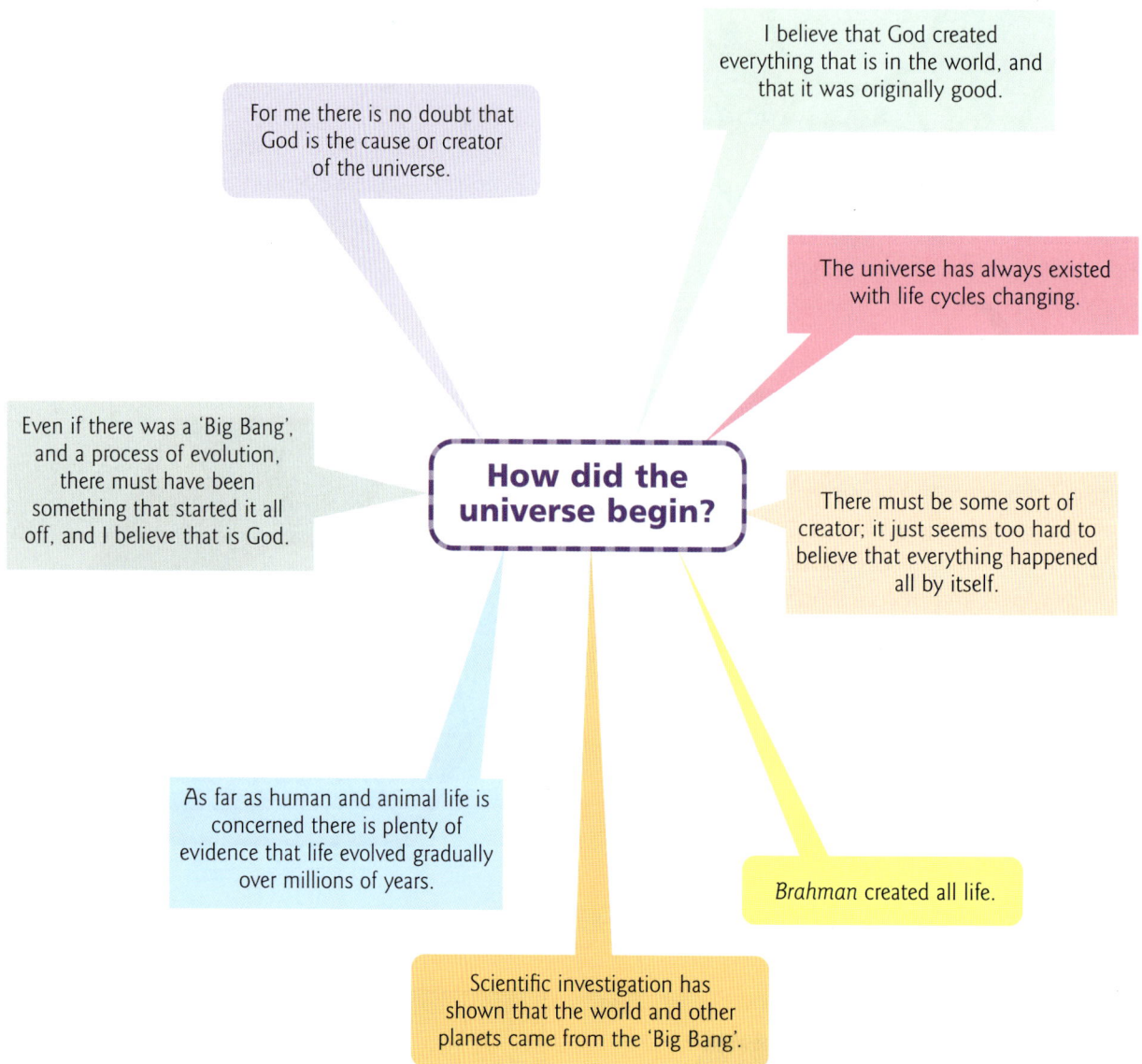

For me there is no doubt that God is the cause or creator of the universe.

I believe that God created everything that is in the world, and that it was originally good.

The universe has always existed with life cycles changing.

Even if there was a 'Big Bang', and a process of evolution, there must have been something that started it all off, and I believe that is God.

How did the universe begin?

There must be some sort of creator; it just seems too hard to believe that everything happened all by itself.

As far as human and animal life is concerned there is plenty of evidence that life evolved gradually over millions of years.

Brahman created all life.

Scientific investigation has shown that the world and other planets came from the 'Big Bang'.

Q 'How the world began does not affect a person's life.' Do you agree? Give reasons or evidence for your answers showing that you have thought about more than one point of view. You must refer to religious beliefs in your answer.

Exam Tip

To gain full marks in evaluation e) questions you should include a range of moral and religious teachings in your arguments and include religious and general specialist language. Look at the points in each of the hands in answer to the question above and use them to help you to answer the question. Work out what specific religious terms from two different religious traditions you could add.

On the one hand …

On the other hand …

- If the world had a purpose in its beginning, that can affect the way a person lives their life.
- Believing that the world was created for a purpose can bring different values into a person's lifestyle.
- Most religions have some teaching about the beginnings of the world, and so these affect believers in considering their beliefs and values.
- Views about how the world began lead to considerations about its future – and these can affect the choices people make.

- Whatever was the cause or beginning was a long time ago and does not affect the way a person lives now.
- Explanations about how the world began do not provide practical help for difficulties in life.
- The choices people make about their lives and actions are made because of needs, situations and family backgrounds.

Issues about the place of humankind in the world

Issues about the place of humankind in the world cover three main areas:
- the place of humankind in the world
- using talents
- stewardship.

Religious teachings on the place of humankind in the world

In the examination, you may be asked questions on religious teachings and attitudes concerning the place of humankind in the world. These are normally b) and d) questions. You need to answer from two different religious traditions. The key religious teachings are outlined below. Many religions agree on the teachings shown in the 'general' box on the scroll.

Key religious teachings: place of humankind in the world

GENERAL
All religions teach that humans are to:
- have sexual relationships and children.
- take responsibility for the world and others in it.
- live lives that are useful and worthwhile.
- use their talents to care for others and the world.

HINDUISM ॐ
Humans are to:
- perfect wisdom, heart and mind.
- live so as to fulfil *dharma*
- practice *ahimsa* (harmlessness).
- amass good *karma*.
- gain *moksha*.

JUDAISM
Humans are to:
- obey God.
- enjoy the world and its fruits/resources.
- look after the earth for God.
- preserve trees.
- live in harmony and care for others.

CHRISTIANITY ✝
Humans are to:
- serve God and live for him.
- obey God.
- enjoy the world and its fruits/resources.
- look after the world for God.

ISLAM ☪
Humans are to:
- live for Allah alone.
- respect other human beings and animals.
- act as *khalifahs* of the planet.

SIKHISM
Humans are to:
- achieve union with God.
- meditate on God's name, focusing heart and mind on God.
- serve others selflessly.
- earn an honest living.

BUDDHISM
Humans are to:
- grow and experience freedom and happiness.
- deepen their understanding of life
- follow the five precepts.
- train the mind to lead to *nirvana*.

Activity

Everyone has talents, things that they are good at doing, like some of the things below:

Musical ability	Sporting skill	Mathematical ability	Artistic talent
Creativity	Acting ability	Practical skills	Building skills
Plumbing skills	Carpentry skills	Good with children	Public speaking

Choose four of the talents above, and say how they might be used in the two religious traditions you have been studying.

Evaluation questions on the place of humankind in the world

There are five issues you should be able to evaluate. These are shown in the diagrams below and on page 60 and are often asked in c) and e) types of questions. Around the five issues in the diagrams are some views (both religious and non-religious) you could include in your answers.

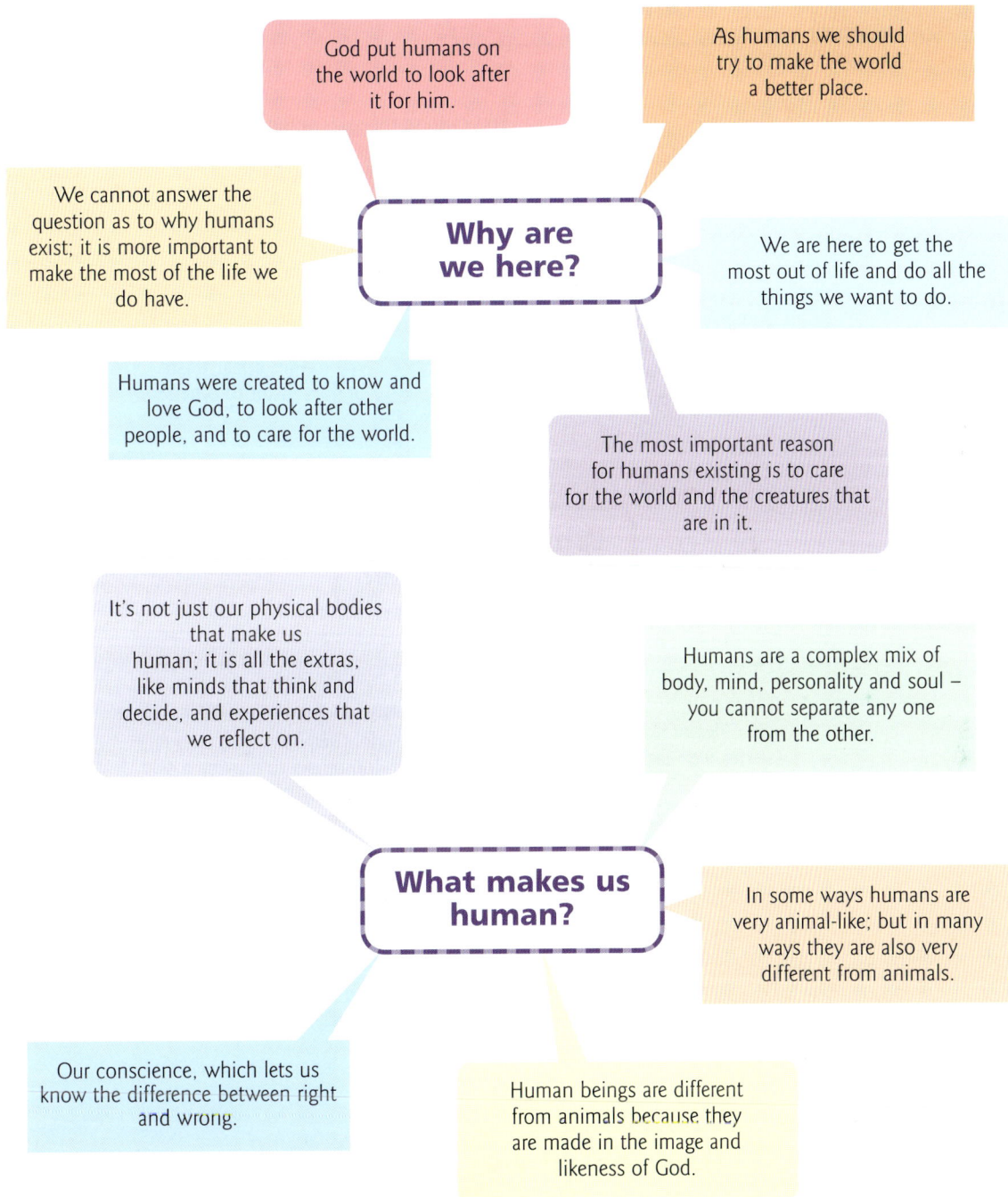

God put humans on the world to look after it for him.

As humans we should try to make the world a better place.

We cannot answer the question as to why humans exist; it is more important to make the most of the life we do have.

Why are we here?

We are here to get the most out of life and do all the things we want to do.

Humans were created to know and love God, to look after other people, and to care for the world.

The most important reason for humans existing is to care for the world and the creatures that are in it.

It's not just our physical bodies that make us human; it is all the extras, like minds that think and decide, and experiences that we reflect on.

Humans are a complex mix of body, mind, personality and soul – you cannot separate any one from the other.

What makes us human?

In some ways humans are very animal-like; but in many ways they are also very different from animals.

Our conscience, which lets us know the difference between right and wrong.

Human beings are different from animals because they are made in the image and likeness of God.

Exam Tip

In questions about the use of talents, try to ensure that you explain how the talents that people have can be used within a religious community, for worshipping, witnessing to others, or helping those who are in need.

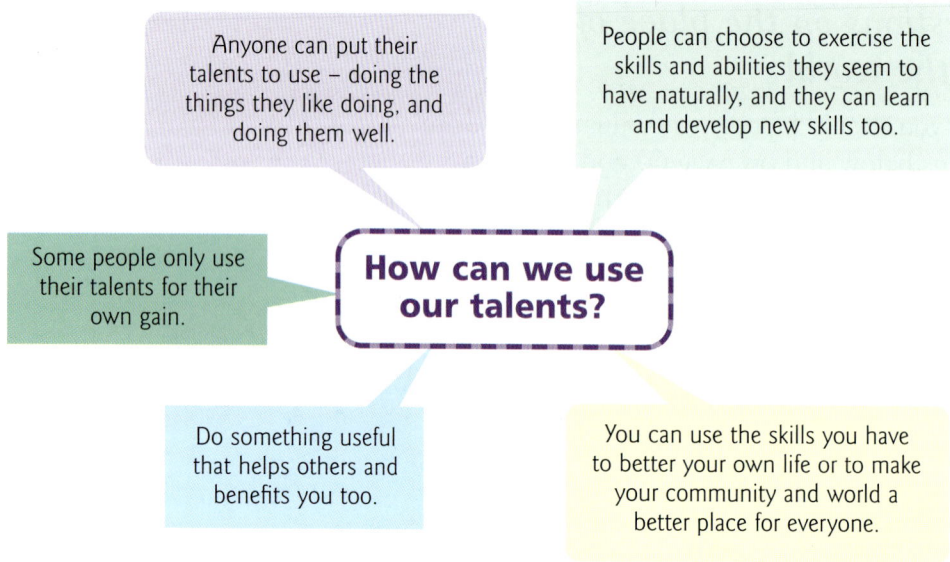

Anyone can put their talents to use – doing the things they like doing, and doing them well.

People can choose to exercise the skills and abilities they seem to have naturally, and they can learn and develop new skills too.

Some people only use their talents for their own gain.

How can we use our talents?

Do something useful that helps others and benefits you too.

You can use the skills you have to better your own life or to make your community and world a better place for everyone.

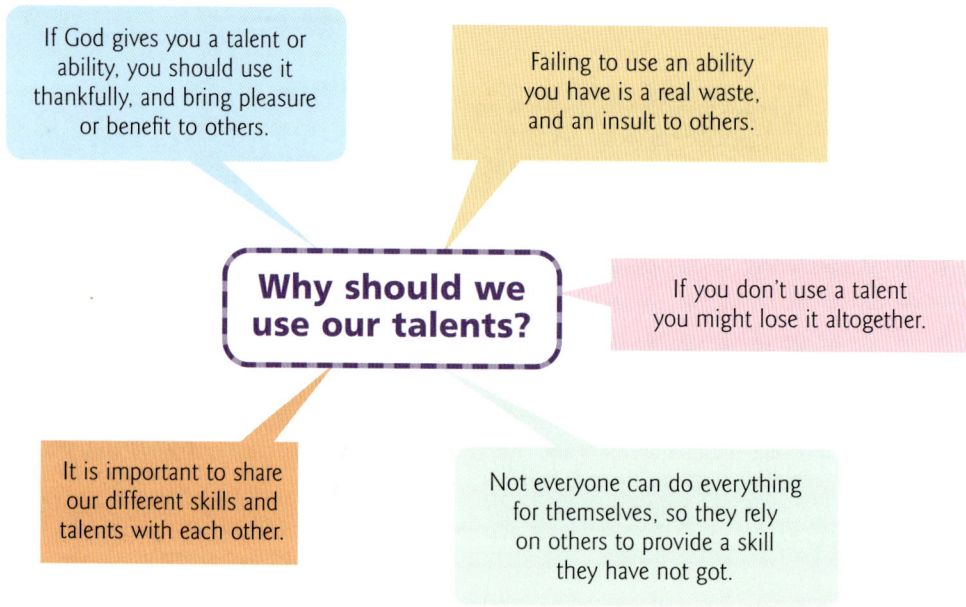

If God gives you a talent or ability, you should use it thankfully, and bring pleasure or benefit to others.

Failing to use an ability you have is a real waste, and an insult to others.

Why should we use our talents?

If you don't use a talent you might lose it altogether.

It is important to share our different skills and talents with each other.

Not everyone can do everything for themselves, so they rely on others to provide a skill they have not got.

The natural resources of the world are there for use to enjoy and make life better.

God has given humans the responsibility of caring for the world, so we should use natural resources wisely.

Being a steward or guardian of the world brings with it the responsibility to be careful in using the resources the world contains.

How should we use natural resources?

We cannot just take; we have to put back too.

Natural resources are not limitless, so we should be careful to ensure that what we use is replaced for the future.

Issues about animal rights

Religious teachings on animal rights

In the examination, you may be asked questions on religious teachings and attitudes concerning animal rights. These are normally b) and d) questions. You need to answer from two different religious traditions. The key religious teachings are outlined below. Many religions agree on the teachings shown in the 'general' box on the scroll.

Key religious teachings: animal rights

GENERAL
All religions have some kind of teaching about the importance of caring for and respecting animal life.

CHRISTIANITY
- Animals are part of God's creation and should be treated with care and respect.
- Although given dominion over animals (in Genesis 1), humans should carry out their stewardship responsibilities carefully and not abuse animals.
- Showing kindness and treating animals well is part of a general lifestyle of gratitude and thankfulness for God's provision.

BUDDHISM
- Everything in creation is interdependent, therefore the way humans treat animals is important.
- Not harming living things is a requirement for all Buddhists.
- Caring for animals helps to improve human life too.

HINDUISM
- All living things have an *atman*, so animals should be treated with respect and care.
- Practising *ahimsa* is also important: not harming any living thing.
- Special honour is given to the cow, which provides milk, butter and fuel and works in the fields.
- Many Hindus are vegetarians.
- 'You must not use your God-given body for killing God's creatures' (Yajur Vedas).

ISLAM
- Animals are part of God's creation and should be respected and cared for.
- Humans were made as *khalifahs* of Allah's world – so caring for animals is part of that responsibility.
- The *Hadith* contains examples of the Prophet being kind to animals.

JUDAISM
- As part of the God-given responsibility of being a steward of the world, Jews are expected to treat animals with concern and compassion.
- Animals should not be abused or harshly treated.
- Even when slaughtering animals for food, this should be done as painlessly as possible.

SIKHISM
- Respect should be shown to all forms of life, including animals.
- The divine spark is in all things, so it is important how you treat them.
- God gave humans the task of being custodians of all that is in the world.

Evaluation questions on animal rights

There is one issue you should be able to evaluate. This is shown in the diagram below and is often asked about in c) and e) types of questions. Around the issue in the diagram below are some views (both religious and non-religious) you could include in your answers.

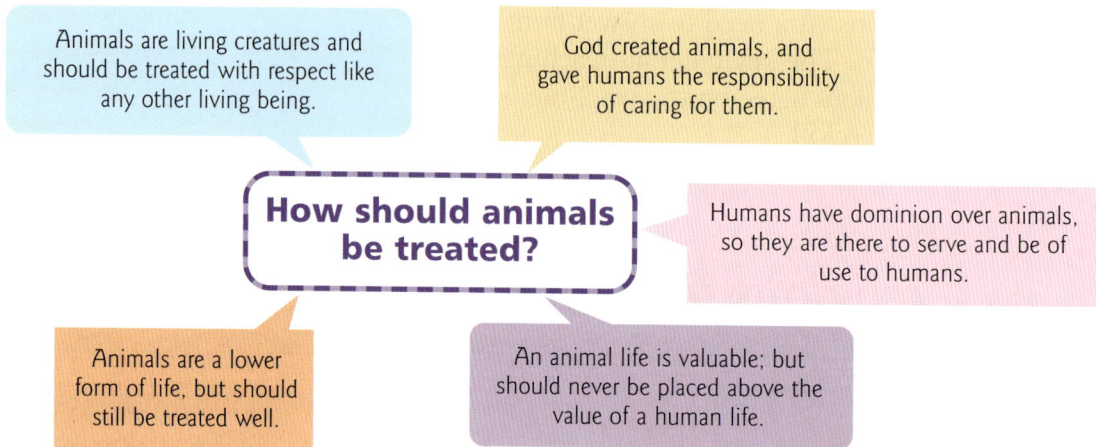

Animals are living creatures and should be treated with respect like any other living being.

God created animals, and gave humans the responsibility of caring for them.

How should animals be treated?

Humans have dominion over animals, so they are there to serve and be of use to humans.

Animals are a lower form of life, but should still be treated well.

An animal life is valuable; but should never be placed above the value of a human life.

Q 'Religious people should campaign for animal rights.' Do you agree? Give reasons or evidence for your answers showing that you have thought about more than one point of view. You must refer to religious beliefs in your answer.

Exam Tip

To gain full marks in evaluation e) questions you should include a range of moral and religious teachings in your arguments and include religious and general specialist language. It is also important to make sure that you show you have thought about more than one point of view. Look at the list of statements below and decide which side to put each statement. Check that you have included religious statements for full marks.

On the one hand ...

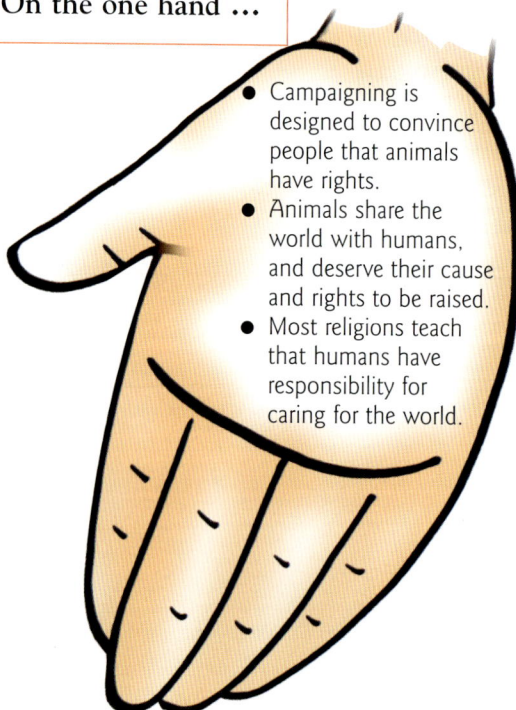

- Campaigning is designed to convince people that animals have rights.
- Animals share the world with humans, and deserve their cause and rights to be raised.
- Most religions teach that humans have responsibility for caring for the world.

On the other hand ...

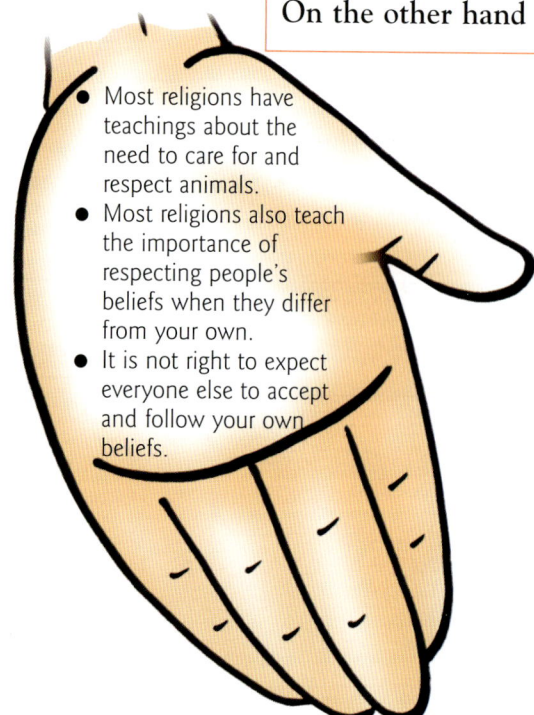

- Most religions have teachings about the need to care for and respect animals.
- Most religions also teach the importance of respecting people's beliefs when they differ from your own.
- It is not right to expect everyone else to accept and follow your own beliefs.

Issues about care for the world and the environment

Religious teachings on care for the world and the environment

In the examination, you may be asked questions on religious teachings and attitudes concerning care for the world and the environment. These are normally b) and d) questions. You would need to answer from two different religious traditions. The key religious teachings are outlined below. Many religions agree to the teachings shown in the 'general' box below.

Key religious teachings: care for the world and the environment

GENERAL
Most religions have ideas about:
- The need to care for the world.
- The importance of protecting and preserving resources and the environment.

CHRISTIANITY ✚
Humans should:
- Live in partnership with God and Creation.
- Exercise responsibility given by God to look after the world.
- Preserve and conserve the resources of the world and the environment.
- Give thanks to God for his provision.

BUDDHISM ☸
- Belief in the interdependence of everything means that Buddhists should care for the world and the environment.
- Taking action to protect the environment makes a difference to future existence.
- Failure to practise harmlessness to all things will affect the future too.

HINDUISM ॐ
- All living beings have *atman* so need to be respected and cared for.
- It is everyone's duty or *dharma* to practise harmlessness and seek good *karma* through good actions.
- It is Shiva's role to destroy things when the time is right, so humans should not try to take over his role.

ISLAM ☪
- Allah gave humans the responsibility to be *khalifahs*, or guardians of his world.
- It is important to preserve the *fitrah*, or balance in the natural world, so humans should use their skills to help keep this balance.
- All that lives or exists in the world is part of Allah's creation, so humans should avoid waste, be kind to animals and respect the earth.

JUDAISM ♉
- God gave humans the responsibility to look after the world he created.
- Thanksgiving is part of caring for the world, and being reminded to enjoy but also to renew.
- It is important to avoid waste and use resources responsibly and carefully.

SIKHISM ☬
- Humans should show respect to nature and all that God provided.
- Humans are custodians of the world for God, and should look after it.
- A good life is one free from waste and needless destruction.

Q In this topic, d)-type questions will often ask you about the IMPACT of religious individuals or groups using their talents to care for the planet. Using the IMPACT formula below should help you to not only remember the key information about the individual or community, but write answers that illustrate the IMPACT of their work.

Look at the IMPACT formula and make sure you have some examples from the two religious traditions you study. Some examples of different religious groups that use their talents to care for the planet are given in the tables below and on page 65. Look them up on the internet for more information about their work.

IMPACT formula

Identify	the correct name of the person or agency
Mention	the religious tradition to which they belong
Précis	the context in which the person or agency is working
Acknowledge	some of the main aspects of their work
Consider	how their work demonstrates the teachings of the religion to which they belong
Tell	of specific examples of long- and short-term projects.

I	Chico Mendes (www.chicomendes.com)	Green Pagodas Project (www.sanghanetwork.org)	Vrindavan (www.mathura-vrindavan.com)
M	**Christian**	**Buddhist**	**Hindu**
P	Brazil – rainforests being cut down	Cambodia – monks helping the community	India – deforestation
A	Organised non-violent resistance	Demonstrating and encouraging healthier and 'greener' lifestyles	Forest revival project
C	Concerned for the lives of people depending on the forests	Practising harmlessness and improving the life of others	Being committed to the principle of *ahimsa*
T	Extractive reserve set up	Well digging, planting trees, improving local practices	Major tree planting, educational projects

Note. The above is *basic* information only. More detail will be required in examination questions.

I Gunug Leuser (www.ifees.org.uk then select 'projects' in left-hand options column)	Jewish National Fund (www.jnf.org)	Khalsa Wood Project (www.lhi.org.uk then select 'East Midlands'. Then 'Nottinghamshire', then 'Sikhism and Khalsa Wood More Than Words')
M Muslim	**Jewish**	**Sikh**
P Aceh–Leuser National Park	Negev–Besor water project	Nottingham
A Cameras placed in rain forest to provide knowledge and training	Reservoir built to provide water	Special woodland project
C Project is called 'Operation Khalifah' – reflecting the guardian role of Islamic belief	As stewards of God's world, helping to provide trees and water to replenish the earth	Serving the community, and helping to preserve the local environment; being custodians for God
T TV channel for teaching and learning about rain forests	Tree planting projects. Water reservoirs built	Planting special woodland and ensuring appropriate facilities for local use

Note. The above is *basic* information only. More detail will be required in examination questions.

Evaluation questions on care for the world and the environment

There is one issue you should be able to evaluate. This is shown in the diagram below and is often asked about in c) and e) types of questions. Around the issue in the diagram below are some views (both religious and non-religious) you could include in your answers.

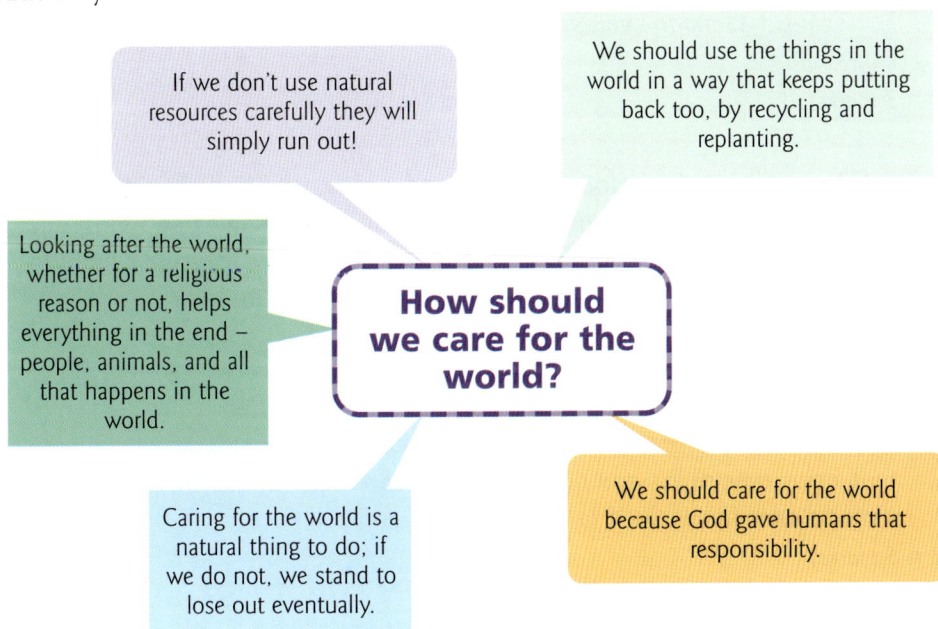

If we don't use natural resources carefully they will simply run out!

We should use the things in the world in a way that keeps putting back too, by recycling and replanting.

Looking after the world, whether for a religious reason or not, helps everything in the end – people, animals, and all that happens in the world.

How should we care for the world?

Caring for the world is a natural thing to do; if we do not, we stand to lose out eventually.

We should care for the world because God gave humans that responsibility.

EXAMINATION PRACTICE

It is important that you understand the structure of the examination paper. This is explained in the Introduction on page 2.

Below are practice questions for each question type in the examination. After each of the questions there is a specimen answer which has been given a mark. Look at the levels of response grids on pages 67–8 and try to improve each answer to get full marks.

Question a) Explain what religious believers mean by 'dominion'. (*2 marks*)

> **Answer** Being over the animals in the world.
>
> (Level 1 = 1 mark)

Question b) Explain how having a religious faith might influence views on the use of our talents. (*4 marks*)

> **Answer** We should use our talents or we will lose them.
>
> (Level 0 = 0 marks)

Question c) 'Life has no built-in purpose; you make it yourself.' Give two reasons why a religious believer might agree or disagree with this statement. (*4 marks*)

> **Answer** Any religious believer would disagree with this because God created the world and all in it – so it must have a purpose.
>
> (Level 2 = 2 marks)

Question d) Explain from **two** different religious traditions the teachings about creation. (*6 marks*)

> **Answer** Christians believe that God created the world, that he created it good, and that there is a purpose to all life in the world. They also believe that human beings have a special relationship to God.
>
> For Sikhs, it is much the same – God created the world and Sikhs should know him.
>
> (Level 3 = 3 marks)

Question e) 'The world is there for us humans to enjoy; that's all that matters.' Do you agree? Give reasons or evidence for your answer, showing that you have thought about more than one point of view. You must include references to religious beliefs in your answer. (*8 marks*)

> **Answer** I partly agree and partly disagree, because as a Christian I believe the world was created by God for humans to enjoy, but also to look after. He gave humans the responsibility of being stewards for him, so we cannot just enjoy everything and do nothing. We can enjoy it, but also have to work hard to care for it. So it is important to do both.
>
> (Level 3 = 5 marks)

Appendix

Levels of Response Grids for Marking

AO1

2 Mark Questions (question a)

Level	Level Descriptor	Mark total
0	No statement of relevant information or explanation.	0
1	A statement of information or explanation which is limited in scope or content.	1
2	An accurate and appropriate explanation of a central teaching, theme or concept.	2

4 Mark Questions (question b)

Level	Level Descriptor	Mark total
0	Makes no link between beliefs and practices.	0
1	A simple link between beliefs and practices.	1
2	An explicit link between beliefs and practices. Limited use of specialist language.	2
3	Analysis showing some awareness and insight into religious facts, ideas, practices and explanations. Uses and interprets a range of religious language and terms.	3
4	Coherent analysis showing awareness and insight into religious facts, ideas, practices and explanations. Uses religious language and terms extensively and interprets them accurately.	4

6 Mark Questions (question d)

Level	Level Descriptor	Mark total
0	A statement of information or explanation which has no relevant content.	0
1	A relevant statement of information or explanation which is limited in scope.	1
2	An accurate account of information or an appropriate explanation of a central teaching, theme or concept. Limited use of religious language.	2
3	An account or explanation indicating knowledge and understanding of key religious ideas, practices, explanations or concepts. Uses and interprets religious language in appropriate context.	3–4
4	A coherent account or explanation showing awareness and insight into religious facts, ideas, practices and explanations. Uses religious language and terms extensively and interprets them accurately.	5–6

AO2

4 Mark Questions (question c)

Level	Level Descriptor	Mark total
0	Makes no relevant point of view.	0
1	A simple, appropriate justification of a point of view.	1
2	**Either:** An expanded justification of one point of view, with appropriate example and/or illustration, which includes religious teaching. **Or:** Two simple, appropriate justifications of a point of view.	2
3	An expanded justification of one point of view, with appropriate example and/or illustration, which includes religious teaching, with a second simple appropriate justification of a point of view (which may be an alternative to the first).	3
4	An expanded justification of two viewpoints, incorporating the religious teaching and moral aspects at issue and their implications for the individual and the rest of society.	4

8 Mark Questions (question e)

Level	Level Descriptor	Mark total
0	Makes no relevant point of view.	0
1	Communicates clearly and appropriately. **Either:** A simple justification of a point of view, possibly linked to evidence or example and making a simple connection between religion and people's lives. **Or:** Two simple appropriate justifications of points of view.	1–2
2	Communicates clearly and appropriately using limited specialist language. **Either:** An expanded justification of one point of view, with appropriate example which includes religious teaching and/or illustration **AND** either a second simple justification. **Or:** Two appropriate justifications of points of view linked to evidence or example, which includes religious teaching.	3–4
3	Communicates clearly and appropriately using and interpreting specialist language. An expanded justification of one point of view, with appropriate examples which includes religious teaching and/or illustration. There is also an adequate recognition of an alternative or different point of view.	5–6
4	Communicates clearly and appropriately using specialist language extensively and thorough discussion, including alternative or different views of the religious teachings and moral aspects at issue and their implications for the individual and the rest of society. Using relevant evidence and religious or moral reasoning to formulate judgement.	7–8

Quality of Written Communication

In all components in questions requiring extended writing (Question 1e), 2e), 3e) and 4e)) candidates will be assessed on the quality of their written communication within the overall assessment of that component.

Mark schemes for all written papers include the following specific criteria for the assessment of written communication:

- Legibility of text; accuracy of spelling, punctuation and grammar; clarity of meaning.

- Selection of a form and style of writing appropriate to purpose and to complexity of subject matter.

- Organisation of information clearly and coherently; use of specialist vocabulary where appropriate.

Glossary

Adultery: sex with someone other than their partner.

Afterlife: (General) the belief that there is some kind of life after the death of the body; a place where souls or spirits go when the body dies.

Agape: Christian love or charity that does not depend on anything.

Agunot: (Jewish) women who have been deserted by their husbands and cannot gain a divorce.

Ahimsa: (Hindu) not killing, non-violence and respect for life.

Akhirah: (Muslim) everlasting life after death – the hereafter.

Allah: (Muslim) the Islamic name for God.

Anand karaj: (Sikh) the wedding ceremony ('ceremony of bliss').

Anandi: (Hindu) that which has no beginning.

Annulment: a declaration by the Church that the marriage never existed.

Artha: (Hindu) economic development: the second aim of life.

Assisted marriages: selection of marriage partner helped by parents and wider family members.

Atman: (Hindu) soul, the real self but can refer to body, mind or soul.

Avatars: (Hindu) 'one who descends' and refers to the 'descents' of Vishnu into the world; sometimes referred to as 'incarnations'.

Awe: completely overwhelmed by a sense of God's presence.

Bet hayyim: (Jewish) cemetery; meaning 'place of the living', or 'house of life'.

Beth Din/Bet Din: (Jewish) group of rabbis who advise Jews on the correct way of living their lives according to the scriptures.

Betrothal: binding with a promise to marry.

Bible: (Christian) the holy book of Christians split into the Old and New Testaments.

Blessings: Giving of favour or grace.

Bodhisattvas: (Buddhist) a person destined for enlightenment, who postpones final attainment of Buddhahood in order to help living beings.

Brahma: (Hindu) a deity, one of the *Trimurti* with Shiva and Vishnu, and in charge of creative power; not to be confused with *Brahman* or Brahmin.

Brahman: (Hindu) the ultimate reality, or the all-pervading reality; from which everything comes and into which everything dissolves.

Buddha, the: (Buddhist) the awakened or enlightened one.

Campaign: a series of actions intended to produce political or social change.

Celibacy: a person who has resolved not to marry.

Chapel: (Christian) The building in which some non-Anglican denominations worship.

Church: (Christian) whole community of Christians; the building in which Christians worship.

Civil disobedience: a form of political protest in which large numbers of people refuse to obey a law.

Civil partnership: a relationship similar to marriage for two people who are of the same sex.

Cohabitation: living together without being married.

Committal: (Christian) words said when a body is being buried or sent for cremation.

Community: a group of people with something in common; faith communities share beliefs and practices.

Covenant: a mutual and solemn agreement or contract.

Creation: making something deliberately for a purpose. Most religions teach that the world was created by God for a purpose.

Creator: one who makes or creates something; many religions talk about a creator who made the universe.

Cremation: the burning of dead bodies.

Deity: generally, a term for God or a supreme being; in Hinduism, an expression of *Brahman* in some form.

Denomination: (Christian) a group of religious believers who have their own organisation and faith.

Dharma: (Hindu) religious duty; the intrinsic quality of the self.

Dignity: having honour and respect.

Dominion: (Christian and Jewish) being in charge of the world for God.

Dukkha: (Buddhist) suffering, ill, unsatisfactoriness, imperfection. The nature of existence according to the first noble truth.

Duty: something that a person is obliged or required to do.

Eightfold path: (Buddhist) teaching of the Buddha about how to reach enlightenment.

Enlightenment: (Buddhist) when a person has got rid of all greed, hatred, delusion, selfishness, ignorance and desire.

Environment: the natural world all about us – plants, insects, animals and humans; religious people may see these as God's creation.

Equal opportunities: a situation in which people have the same opportunities in life as other people, without being treated in an unfair way because of their race, sex, sexuality, religion or age.

Eros: earthly or sexual love.

Eternal life: a life that has no end or time limit. In Christianity, refers to the gift of life after death that comes through belief in Jesus.

Evangelise: to tell people about a religion in order to persuade them to become members of that religion.

Faithful: showing loyalty.

Fitrah: (Muslim) balance in the natural world.

Five Ks: (Sikh) the five sacred Sikh symbols prescribed by Guru Gobind Singh commonly known as the Five Ks because they start with letter K.

Five Pillars: (Muslim) Fundamental tenets of Islamic belief and practice.

Five precepts: (Buddhist) principles or rules to follow for right behaviour and spiritual progress.

Ganesha: (Hindu) a Hindu deity who removes obstacles.

Get: (Jewish) divorce.

God: diety or supreme being; creator of the universe; one who should be worshipped.

Golden Rule: rule common to many religions which stated you should treat others as you wish to be treated.

Gurdwara: (Sikh) Sikh place of worship.

Gurmukh: (Sikh) one who lives by the Guru's teaching; God centred.

Guru Granth Sahib: (Sikh) collection of Sikh scriptures given its final form by Guru Gobind Singh.

Haram: (Muslim) anything unlawful or not permitted.

Havan: (Hindu) ceremony in which offerings of ghee and grains are made into fire.

Human rights: the rights that everyone should have in a society, including the right to express opinions about the government or to have protection from harm.

Humanae vitae: (Christian) an encyclical written by Pope Paul VI reaffirming the teaching of the Roman Catholic Church regarding abortion, contraception, and other issues pertaining to human life.

Humanity: caring for other human beings through prayer and action.

Iblis: (Muslim) the being who defied Allah, and later became the tempter of all human beings (*Shaytan* – the devil).

Iddah: (Muslim) the waiting period before a divorced or widowed woman can remarry.

Ik Onkar: (Sikh) the first phrase of the *Mool Mantar* ('There is only one God'). Also a symbol to decorate Sikh objects.

Illusory: (Buddhist) deceptive or false.

Image of God: (Christian) the belief that humans are created in the image and likeness of God; they share something of God's character.

Imam: (Muslim) a person who leads communal prayers.

Influence: exercising power.

Interment: (Christian) another word for burial.

Ishta-dev: (Hindu) chosen deity.

Jesus: (Christian) the central figure of Christian history and devotion. The second part of the Trinity.

Justice: just conduct or fairness.

Karma: (Hindu) action; often used to refer to the law of cause and effect.

Karma, collective: (Buddhist) when the effects of *karma* are shared by more than one individual.

Ketubah: (Jewish) a document that defines rights and obligations within Jewish marriages.

Khalifah: (Muslim) successor, or custodian (of the earth), inheritor.

Kiddushin: (Jewish) betrothal. *Kiddushin* is accomplished beneath the *chuppah* (wedding canopy) with the exchange of rings.

Kirat karna: (Sikh) earning one's livelihood by one's own effort.

Langar: (Sikh) the *gurdwara* dining hall and the food served in it.

Lust: desire for sexual indulgence or passion.

Mahr: (Muslim) dowry or bridal gifts.

Mandap: (Hindu) canopy often used in a marriage ceremony.

Mandir: (Hindu) temple.

Materialism: The view that money, wealth and objects are very important.

Media: radio, television, newspapers, the internet, and magazines, considered as a group.

Messiah: (Jewish) the promised saviour sent by God.

Metta: (Buddhist) loving kindness; a pure love which isn't grasping or possessive.

Mezuzah: (Jewish) a scroll placed on doorposts of Jewish homes containing a section from the Torah and enclosed in a decorative case.

Middle way: (Buddhist) the way that leads to cessation of suffering.

Mitzvah: (Jewish) duty; often used to describe good deeds.

Moksha: (Hindu) ultimate liberation from the continuous cycle of birth and death.

Mosque: (Muslim) place of prostration; often called a *masjid*.

Mukti: (Sikh) union with God.

Murti: (Hindu) form or image or deity used as a focus of worship.

Natural resources: (General) raw materials – air, land, water, wood, natural gas, oil, minerals, wildlife, etc. – that are used by humans; some are renewable others non-renewable.

Nikkah: (Muslim) marriage contract.

Nirvana: (Hindu) the cessation of material existence. (Buddhist) the blowing out of the fires of greed, hatred and ignorance, and the state of perfect peace that follows.

Omnipotent: all-powerful; often used as a descriptor of one of the characteristics of God in Christianity and Judaism.

Omniscient: all-knowing; often used as a descriptor of one of the characteristics of God in Christianity and Judaism.

Ordained: making someone a priest or religious leader.

Philia: (Christian) Greek word for love of friends, or friendship.

Polygamy: having more than one wife at any one time.

Pray: an attempt to contact God usually through words but also through silence and icons.

Precepts, five: (Buddhist) principles or rules to follow for right behaviour and spiritual progress.

Prejudge: to come to a view before having full knowledge.

Priest: (Christian) ordained person who leads prayer and worship in a church.

Prophet Muhammad: (Muslim) The final prophet.

Puja: (Hindu) worship.

Qur'an: (Muslim) The divine book revealed to the Prophet Mohammad.

Rabbi: (Jewish) an ordained Jewish teacher.

Raheguru: (Sikh) 'Wonderful Lord', a Sikh name for God.

Rebirth: (Buddhist) the *kammic* energy of a person setting another life into being.

Redemption: (Christian) delivered or freed from sin by being 'redeemed' or 'bought back'.

Reincarnation: generally being born into another body or being after death. (Hindu) Transmigration of the *atman* from one body to another.

Requiem Mass: (Christian, Roman Catholic) celebrating Mass or Holy Communion for the dead person at a funeral.

Responsibility: duties you should carry out such as looking after others and the world.

Resurrection: generally coming back to life again. (Christian) A central belief in the coming back to life of Jesus and also of all believers. (Jewish) Many Jews also believe in the coming back to life of the dead.

Revelation: something shown or explained that was previously hidden. Many religions have revealed truths.

Sacrament: (Christian) an outward sign of an inward blessing.

Sacred: consecrated or holy.

Sacred texts: holy books and teachings.

Sadaqah: (Muslim) voluntary payment or good action for charity.

Samskara: (Hindu) a rite of passage.

Sangha: (Buddhist) community or assembly.

Sargun: (Sikh) God being seen as everywhere and in everything.

Sat Nam: (Sikh) 'Eternal Reality', a Sikh name for God.

Seva: (Sikh) service or work without the expectation of reward.

Shabbat: (Jewish) day of spiritual renewal beginning on Friday at sunset and terminating at nightfall on Saturday.

Shema: (Jewish) major Jewish prayer affirming belief in one God; it is found in the Torah.

Shiva: (Hindu) a god, one of the *Trimurti* with Brahma and Vishnu; the name means kindly or auspicious.

Soul: the part of human nature that is not just physical, and that lives on after the body has died. Also that part of humans that allows them to relate to God and to worship.

Stewardship: to guard over something for the real owner; a God-given responsibility to manage or control the earth.

Storge: (Christian) Greek word for the love of things – objects, animals.

Story of the Good Samaritan: (Christian) a parable Jesus told.

Subhah: (Muslim) string of beads used to count recitations in worship.

Sukkot: (Jewish) one of three biblical pilgrim festivals; *Sukkot* is celebrated in the autumn.

Symbolism: something that points to or explains something else; many religions have symbolic actions.

Synagogue: (Jewish) a building for Jewish public prayer, study and assembly.

Talents: Something that a person is good at doing – a skill or ability.

Tawhid: (Muslim) belief in the oneness of Allah – absolute monotheism as practised in Islam.

Tikkun Olam: (Jewish) care for the world and the environment.

Torah: (Jewish) the five books of Moses.

Transcendent: something that surpasses all human knowledge and experience. Often used as a descriptor of one of the characteristics of God in Christianity.

Trimurti: (Hindu) the three deities Brahma, Vishnu and Shiva, who personify and control the three functions of creation, preservation and destruction.

Trinity: (Christian) three persons in one God – God the Father, God the Son and God the Holy Spirit.

Tu B'Shevat: (Jewish) a festival, usually in late January or early February, that marks 'the New Year of the Trees'. Often trees are planted at this time.

Tzedeka: (Jewish) an act of charity.

Ummah: (Muslim) community; the Worldwide community of Muslims.

Vishnu: (Hindu) a god, one of the *Trimurti* with Brahma and Shiva.

Vocation: divine call for a career.

Vows: solemn promises or oaths made before God or other deities.

Yahrzeit: (Jewish) 'year time'; anniversary of a death.

Zaccheus: (Christian) the story of Zaccheus is in Luke's gospel. He was a chief tax collector who was disliked by the public but Jesus spoke to him to show that people shouldn't discriminate against others.

Zakah: (Muslim) one of the Five Pillars; giving up wealth to the poor and needy